TAIJI QUAN:
48 Forms

Compiled by
the Chinese Wushu Association

FOREIGN LANGUAGES PRESS   BEIJING

First Edition   2001

Home Page:
http://www.flp.com.cn
E-mail Addresses:
Info@flp.com.cn
Sales@flp.com.cn

ISBN 7-119-01964-3

©Foreign Languages Press, Beijing, 2001
Published by Foreign Languages Press
24 Baiwanzhuang Road, Beijing 100037, China

Distributed by China International Book Trading Corporation
35 Chegongzhuang Xilu, Beijing 100044, China

Printed in the People's Republic of China

Contents

I. Characteristics

For centuries, Taiji Quan has been popular among the Chinese people for its tonic effects and as an aid to improved physical fitness. It is a treasured cultural legacy created by the working people of China.

These 48 Forms of Taiji Quan have all the special features of the traditional schools of Taiji Quan—the spirit of relaxation, softness, smoothness, circularity and continuity. Their practice calls for a quiet mind, a relaxed body, consciousness-guided movements, and combination of hardness and softness. These forms are mainly based on the Yang Style Taiji Quan, but also draw upon the strong points and techniques of other styles. The exercises are smooth, circular, balanced, complete, lively and simple.

The 48 Forms of Taiji Quan have the following characteristics:

(I) Essentials

The entire set has 48 forms of movements, including the three hand forms: fist, palm and hook; nine stances: bow step, empty step, crouch step, cross-legged resting stance, T-step, semi-horse stance step, one-leg stance, standing stance with feet apart, and side bow stance; four leg techniques: toe kick, heel kick, slap kick, and lotus kick; and various hand techniques and different kinds of footwork. These movements represent the main contents of Taiji Quan, and omit repetitions of movements in the traditional routines. Generally speaking, a single movement is used once each in the left and right forms.

(II) Circular Movements

The 48 Forms include not only the vertical circular movements of Yang Style Taiji Quan, but also the horizontal circular movements of the traditional routines of Wu Style and Sun Style Taiji Quan. These include the single whip, the waving of hands like cloud, piercing and rubbing movements in the stroking and pushing forms, and the circular connecting movements for downward striking with a forward step, shuttling to the left and to the right, and the right heel kick. All these movements are circular, smooth, and well coordinated. In the footwork, the 48 Forms include the backward step and follow-up step of the Wu and Sun schools of Taiji Quan to make the footwork more flexible on the basis of the steady, light and nimble movements of the Yang Style. In forming patterns, the set calls for the full extension of the parts of the body in an integrated manner. In the forms of Leaning Obliquely, Standing on One Leg to Mount Tiger, White Snake Sticks out Its Tongue, and Turning Body with Big Strokes, for example, the movements both demonstrate the characteristics of Wushu and present excellent artistic patterns.

(III) Balance and Completeness

In the 48 Forms attention is paid to the completeness and balance of the movements. In the forms of Single Whip, Waving Hands like Clouds, and Strike, Parry and Punch, the symmetrical right forms have been added, based on the left forms, thus correcting the imbalance of movements in some traditional routines. For the legs, the set includes 29 bow steps (15 left bow steps and 14 right bow steps), 12 empty steps (seven left empty steps and five right empty steps), six crouch steps, and six one-leg stances (three for each leg). This helps balance the weight on the legs. Also, many fist techniques are used and account for one third of the hand movements, thus exceeding the limit of "five fist strikes in Taiji Quan" of many traditional routines.

(IV) Rational Arrangement

The whole set is divided into six parts with two climaxes. The first part includes seven forms with stress on the basic hand forms, hand techniques, stances and footwork. The principal form is Stroke and Push. The second part includes the eighth through the 13th forms, in which changeovers in footwork and body techniques are more flexible. The principal form is Turn to Push Palms. The third part includes the 14th through the 19th forms, which make up the first climax of the set of exercises. The principal form is Pat Foot to Subdue Tiger. The fourth part includes the 20th through the 28th forms and the principal form is Kick with Left and Right Foot. The fifth part includes the 29th through the 36th forms and the principal form is Work at Shuttles on Both Sides. The fourth and fifth parts lay stress on balance, pliability and toughness, and the coordination of the movements. The movements in the Kick with Right and Left Feet, Kick with Heel, Waving Hands Like Clouds and Works at Shuttles forms, for example, all set high standards for correct bodily execution. The sixth part includes the last 12 forms when the final climax of the entire set is reached. It includes three hand forms, seven stances, one outside kick, and various hand techniques, footwork and body techniques. The key forms in this part are Turn Body with Big Strokes and Turn Body for Lotus Leg Swing. The set begins with the White Crane Spreads Its Wings and closes with Warding off, Stroking, Pushing and Pressing, and Cross Hands.

(V) User-Friendly

The 48 Forms are linked up with the well-known 24 simplified forms of Taiji Quan, both in content and style. The 48 Forms include as many familiar movements and positions as possible. Some of the forms and movements have a higher degree of difficulty and include movements that release force, such as the Pat Foot to Subdue Tiger and Strike with Hidden Fist. Different methods of practice and ranges of movement are specified for people of different physiques and preferences. We hope this will create conditions favorable for popularizing the 48 Forms.

II. Basic Technical Essentials

(I) Hand Movements

1. Fist: The fingers are doubled into the palm and the thumb doubled inward across the forefinger and the middle finger.

2. Palm: The fingers are slightly bent and apart, the palm slightly cupped, and the radial between the thumb and forefinger curved.

3. Hook: The tips of the fingers are held together, wrist bent.

All hand movements must be kept natural, avoiding stiffness. The fist must not be clenched too tightly, the fingers not too stiff or bent too softly, and the wrist should be relaxed.

(II) Hand Techniques

1. Ward off: Curve the arm, move the forearm forward from below to block and ward off, and place it in front of the body, palm inside at shoulder level. Focus the force on the outside of the forearm.

2. Stroke: Bend both arms slightly, palms obliquely facing each other, and curve the palms while turning the waist, from in front of the body backward to the sides of the body, or to behind the sides of the body.

3. Push: Push both arms forward together, with the rear hand close to the inside of the front hand. After pushing, form the arms into a circle to a height between the shoulder and the chest. Focus the force on the palm fingers of the rear hand and the forearm of the front hand.

4. Press: Push and press both palms forward from behind. After pressing, keep the wrists at a height between the shoulder and the chest, palm forward, fingers up, arms slightly bent and elbows relaxed and dropped. The pressing should be coordinated with the bowing of the legs and the relaxing of the waist.

5. Thrust fist(s): Turn and thrust the fist(s) forward from the

waist. After thrusting, keep the fist eye and the thumb at a height between the shoulder and the crotch, arm slightly bent and elbow not too stiff. Focus the force on the fist face.

6. Plunge downward: Plunge the fist from above forward and downward. After plunging, keep the fist face forward down, with the thumb to one side. Focus the force on the fist face.

7. Sweep the fist inward: Sweep the fist horizontally from sideways below obliquely upward. Bend the arm slightly, fist eye obliquely up. Focus the force on the fist face.

8. Chop the fist: Chop the fist from above forward, fist center obliquely up at head level. Focus the force on the fist back.

9. Thread the fist: Extend the fist forward from the inner side of the other hand or the thigh.

10. Swing the fist with bent arm: First bend the arm and stretch it to raise the fist from below forward or forward down to strike. After striking, keep the fist center down, not higher than shoulder level, or lower than crotch level.

11. Hold the palms: Keep the palms facing each other or stagger them slightly as if holding a ball in front of the body or by the side of the body, upper hand not higher than the shoulder and lower hand about waist level. Keep the palms in a round shape and arms curved. Relax the shoulders and drop the elbows.

12. Part palms: Move the palms obliquely apart, one forward and the other backward, or one up and the other down. After parting, put the front hand in front of the head or the body, and press the rear hand to the hips. Bend the arms in a slight curve.

13. Circle palm: Circle the palms horizontally in front of the knees to the hips, palm down.

14. Push palm: Push the palms forward from above the shoulders or in front of the chest, palm forward and fingers up, fingers not higher than the eyebrows or lower than the shoulders. Bend the arms in a slight curve. The elbows should not be stiff or straight.

15. Thread palm: Thrust the palm forward over the inner side of the other arm, or the thigh.

16. Wave hands like clouds: Cross palms in front of the body to draw vertical circles to both sides, fingers not higher than the

head or lower than the crotch. Wave the palms like clouds.

17. Swing the palms: Swing the palms from below forward or forward down, palm upward or forward, not higher than the chest or lower than the crotch.

18. Palm block: Bend the arm and lift it up to block obliquely in front of the forehead, palm obliquely outward.

19. Open palms: Open the palms, move them apart, one upward and the other down, and prop them up powerfully and symmetrically.

20. Press palm: Press the palm downward, with the thumb inward and the palm down.

21. Hold up palm: Hold the palm up from below.

22. Pluck palm: Pull and stroke the palm obliquely from front downward.

23. Beat: Use the palm to beat obliquely outward.

24. Lean. The shoulders, back, or upper arms release the force outward obliquely.

All hand techniques should be executed in curved lines, with forearms turned correspondingly, not straight or stiff. They should be coordinated with the body techniques and footwork. After the arms are stretched out, the shoulders and elbows should be relaxed and dropped, wrists relaxed and flexible, and palms fully extended. Nothing should be stiff or soft. The force points of the hand techniques are mainly for attack and defense. Attention should be paid to consciousness rather than to force. Stiff force should not be used intentionally.

(III) Stances

1. Bow step: With feet apart, bend the front leg, knee and toes almost on a vertical line, toes straight forward. Straighten the rear leg naturally, toes obliquely forward at 45°-60°. Keep both feet on the floor.

2. Empty step: Squat with bent knees, heel and hips forming a vertical line. Tiptoe obliquely forward with the foot entirely on the floor. Bend the front leg slightly, ball, heel or entire foot on the floor.

3. Crouch stance: Bend one leg and squat fully, with the foot

on the floor, toes slightly outward. Straighten the other leg naturally, close to the ground, foot on the floor and toes inward.

4. Stand on one leg: Stand on one leg, slightly bent. Bend the other leg and raise it in front of the body.

5. Stand with feet apart: Stand with feet apart to shoulder width, parallel to each other, legs straight or bent in the squating position.

6. Cross-legged stance: Cross the legs to squat down, rear knee close to the back of the front knee. Keep the front foot on the floor, tiptoe outward, ball of the rear foot on the floor and toes forward.

7. Semi-horse stance: Keep the front foot straight forward, and the rear foot horizontally outward, two or three feet between them and both feet fully on the floor. Bend both legs, with body weight slightly on the rear leg.

8. Toe step: Squat with one leg, foot on the floor. Bend and withdraw the other leg, foot by the inner side of the supporting foot or 10 cm before or behind the foot side, with the ball of the front foot touching the floor.

9. Side bow step: Stand with feet apart to the width of the bow step with toes of both foot forward. Squat with one leg, knee and tiptoe forming a vertical line. Straighten the other leg.

All stances must be executed naturally and steadily. Combining emptiness and solidness. The hips should be drawn in, and the knees relaxed, buttocks held in and feet inward. The distance between the feet should be neither too big nor too small. Especially when executing the twist step, the feet should not be placed on the same line so that the waist and hips are relaxed, the energy flows, and the body weight is balanced.

(IV) Footwork

1. Forward step: Move the rear foot one step forward, or the front foot half a step forward.

2. Backward step: Move the front foot one step backward.

3. Withdrawing step: Move the front foot, or the rear foot, half a step backward.

4. Advance steps: Move both feet one step forward, one after

the other.

5. Follow-up step: Move the rear foot half a step forward.

6. Side step: Move one feet parallel and sideways continuously.

7. Front cross step: Move one foot across the supporting foot and land it on the other side.

8. Back cross step: Move the foot behind the supporting foot to the other side.

9. Grinding step: Pivot on the heel, toes outward or inward; and pivot on the ball of the front foot, heel out.

All steps should be light, nimble, and steady, and should combine emptiness with solidness. In advancing, land the heel first, and in retreating, land the ball first, moving in cat-like steps. The feet must not rise or fall clumsily, slowly, or heavily. They should be kept properly apart, whether longitudinally or latitudinally. The turning on the heel or ball of foot should be appropriate so that the body weight is balanced and the posture is natural. Straighten the legs naturally and avoid stiff knees.

(V) Leg Techniques

1. Kick with heel: Stand firmly with the supporting leg slightly bent, bend the other leg and raise it, and swing the shank upward, toes flexed, to kick out with the heel to above waist level.

2. Toe kick: Stand firmly with the supporting leg slightly bent, swing the shank upward, instep flat, and kick out with the toe to above waist level.

3. Slap kick: Stand firmly with the supporting leg slightly bent, swing the other leg to kick upward, instep flat, and pat the instep in front of the forehead with the palm.

4. Lotus kick: Stand firmly with the supporting leg slightly bent, kick upward with the other leg from the other side, swing it in the shape of a Chinese fan outside in front of the body, instep flat, and use both hands to pat the insteps, one after another, in front of the forehead.

In executing the leg techniques, the supporting leg must be firm, the knee must not be stiff, the hip joints must be relaxed, and the torso kept upright. Don't lower the head or bend the body, and don't bend forward or backward, or to the right or to the left.

(VI) Body Form, Body Work, and Eye Techniques

1. Body form

(1) Head: Keep the neck straight and the head up. Do not slant or shake the head.

(2) Neck: Keep the neck upright naturally. Do not stiffen the muscles.

(3) Shoulders: Relax and drop the shoulders. Do not shrug, or stretch them backward, or hold them forward.

(4) Elbows: Drop and relax the elbows, and bend them naturally. Do not stiffen them or lift them up.

(5) Chest: Relax the chest and hold it in slightly. Do not thrust the chest out or hold it in too much.

(6) Back: Straighten the back. Don't be humpback.

(7) Waist: Keep the waist relaxed and natural. Do not arch it or hold it out.

(8) Backbone: Keep the backbone upright and straight. Do not twist it to either side.

(9) Buttocks: Keep the buttocks in. Do not thrust it out or sway it.

(10) Hips: Keep them relaxed, upright and in. Do not stiffen them or thrust them to either side.

(11) Knees: Bend, stretch and relax the knees naturally. Do not stiffen them.

2. Body work

Keep the body upright and comfortable, turn the body naturally, flexibly, evenly and steadily. The movements are executed with the waist as the pivot to move the limbs in unison. Body movements should not be stiff, stagnant, flighty or unsteady. The body should not be bent forward or backward, or rise or fall irregularly.

3. The Eyes

Taiji Quan requires concentration of the mind, the use of consciousness to guide the movements, and a natural look. In the fixed position, the eyes should look straight ahead or at the hands.

When changing positions, the eyes, hand techniques, and body work should be coordinated.

(VII) Essential Points for the Execution of Movements

1. Relax the body, keep calm, and breathe naturally. All parts of the body should be natural and relaxed, and no clumsy force should be used. Concentrate the mind and remain quiet to guide the movements. Breathe naturally, smoothly, deeply and evenly, in coordination with the movements and the application of force. The general rule is: inhale lightly and exhale solidly, inhale when the mouth opens, and exhale when the mouth closes. Do not hold the breath in a forced manner.

2. The movements should be curved with a clear distinction between emptiness and solidness. The change from movement to movement should be circular, not straight, and should not be stiff or rigid. The body weight should be shifted firmly and stably, with a clear difference between emptiness and solidness. The shift of weight should be smooth and decisive.

3. The upper and lower limbs should move in unison, circularly and fully. The movements must be executed with the waist as the pivot to move the limbs in unison. Avoid disharmony between the hands and feet and between the waist and the rest of the body. The movement of force should be uninterrupted.

4. Execute the movements evenly, continuously, smoothly and calmly. The movements should be closely connected, soft, continuous and flowing. The speed should be even. Be sure to avoid uneven movements of the several parts of the body. When the movements release force or involve the patting of the feet, the speed can be changed, but the connections should be natural, and the manner should be integral.

5. Keep the movements light and steady, and combine hardness with softness. The application of force should be light, flexible, firm and steady. It should be externally soft and internally solid. Hardness and softness should be combined. The release of power should originate from the waist and legs, and

should be focused on the hands. The movements are elastic and flexible, with softness dwelling in hardness.

III. Steps for Practice

To practice Taiji Quan, just as with any other sports, you must acquire a good foundation from the very beginning, gradually improve your skills, and finally perfect them.

Roughly speaking, learning to practice Taiji Quan may be divided into three stages. In the first stage you should lay a good foundation in the positions and movements. Beginners should first acquire a clear understanding of the basics including hand forms, hand techniques, stances, footwork, body form, body work, leg work and eye techniques. Make sure your positions are correct and the movements are smooth and soft. In the second stage, you should begin to grasp the correct method of how to change from movement to movement, and the characteristics of the movements. Make sure that the movements are continuous, well-connected, circular and coordinated, with the limbs moving in unison. In the third stage, emphasis should be put on the application of force, consciousness, and the combination of breathing and movements. Make sure that the movements are executed lightly and firmly, that hardness is combined with softness and the mind, and that energy and force are integrated both internally and externally.

A brief description of the essential points for learning the 48 Forms of Taiji Quan is as follows:

In the first stage, for the foundation work, attention should be paid to the following points:

(I) Correctness: In learning to practice Taiji Quan you must, first of all, keep your body upright and comfortable, and take the correct position. When raising the head and straightening the neck, dropping the shoulders and elbows, relaxing the waist and holding in the buttocks, special attention should be paid to keeping the spine straight and the shoulders and hips relaxed and flat to ensure an upright torso. The positions for the other parts of the body should also be executed earnestly and correctly as required. As a matter of fact, ignorance of the essential points for any one part of the body will lead to a deformation in the positions of the other parts. For example, if the buttocks protrude, the waist will be affected, the chest will be thrust out, and the abdomenal muscles will become tense, causing errors in the execution of the movements. Therefore, the beginners must not seek quick progress or learn hastily and carelessly.

(II) Stability: To ensure that the torso is upright and comfortable, it is first of all necessary to keep the lower limbs stable. The stances and footwork are the foundation of good positions and movements. If the steps are too small and too narrow or the positions and angles of the feet are not correct, and the distinction between emptiness and solidness is not clear while excuting the movements, instability of the body will result. Therefore, beginners must first have a clear understanding of the stances and footwork. You can properly grasp the timing for the change of body weight by practicing the stances and different steps separately. Or you can practice the different leg techniques (heel, toe, and side kick) and do more exercises to improve the pliability of the waist. This can also increase lower-limb strength and improve the stability of the movements.

(III) Relaxation: Beginners should pay attention to relaxation when executing the movements. The body parts should be fully extended and the movements should be soft and natural. Beginners are likely to use clumsy force and become unnecessarily nervous. In laying the foundation, the body parts must be relaxed and the movements must be soft. Strive to overcome nervousness and stiff movement.

(IV) Lightness and softness: In order to acquire lightness, slowness, softness and gentleness required by Taiji Quan movements, beginners should do the exercises slowly and softly, and apply the force lightly and evenly. Generally speaking, slow movements and light force at the beginning help make correct movements at the right pace and avoid incorrect force application.

In the second stage, a firm grasp of the rules of Taiji Quan movements should be stressed. In order to demonstrate the characteristics of Taiji Quan, we must focus on the following points:

(I) Continuity: After a certain foundation has been laid for the positions and movements, the next step is to make the entire exercise continuous. All movements should be well connected with those preceeding and those following. The whole set of exercises should be done without interruption, like flowing water and floating clouds. The end of one exercise is the exact beginning of the following one. For example, at the beginning, the four movements of warding off, stroking, pushing, and pressing can be practiced separately. After you are skilled in these exercises, you should connect them fluidly and practice them as one. Although there should be a certain sense of rhythm between two exercises (as though a slight pause after one exercise is finished), the one following should be started immediately as though the previous exercise seemed to pause, but did not pause. The whole set of exercises should be well connected and done continuously without breaks. There should be no pause.

(II) Coordination: Taiji Quan is an exercise for the whole human body. It calls for the movement of all parts at the same time, and good coordination among them. In executing the "cloud hand," for example, when the waist is turned, it drives the arms out to draw circles in the air with the palms turning inside and outside together continuously with the movement of the buttocks, and the legs supporting the entire body to move and turn to the left or to the right, while the head also turns naturally with the torso. At the same time, the eyes look at the upper hand. In this way, the whole body moves in coordination, with close cooperation between all the body's elements.

(III) Circularity: Taiji Quan movements are formed by various arcs and curves. Once this rule is grasped, you can consciously avoid straight-line movements, dead turns, and right angles, and make your movements circular. The waist is pivotal for generating the movement of the limbs. Only when the waist is used as the pivot, is it possible to make hand movements and foot work circular, smooth, light, gentle and flexible.

The third stage is known by some as the stage for "training

the mind, energy and power." In this stage, attention should be given to the following points:

(I) Make a clear distinction between emptiness and solidness, and combine softness with hardness.

In Wushu exercises the contradictary changes are often called the changes between the empty and the solid. In Taiji Quan as a whole the end of a movement in the final position is solid and the process of changing the movement is empty. In the separate exercises, the main supporting leg is the "solid" and the auxiliary supporting leg, or the moving and changing leg, is the "empty" one; and the arm which demonstrates the main content of the exercise is the "solid," while the auxiliary and supporting hand is the "empty" one. When the empty and the solid are clearly defined, in applying the force there should be both tension and relaxation. The solid movements and parts call for heavy and substantial force, while the empty movements and parts call for gentle and implicit force. For example, when the exercise comes to the final position or is nearing the finish, the waist and joints should be relaxed and stable. When the exercises are changed, the joints of the whole body should be relaxed and invigorated. When the movements of the upper limbs change from empty to solid, the forearms should be firm, and the palms should be fully extended, with the fingers relaxed and the wrists flat. The fists should be clenched first loosely and then tightly. When changing from empty to solid, the movement of the forearm should be gentle with the fists loosely clenched. In conjunction with the changing movements between the empty and the solid, there is both softness and force and tension and relaxation, alternating one with the other. The exercises are light, gentle and firm, with the equal application of force for all movements.

(II) Continuous movements and integral force.

Apart from the combination of softness and hardness, Taiji Quan calls for the uninterrupted application of even and integral force. Interrupted application of force means interruption, discontinuity, pause, and sudden change in the application of force. To ensure the continuous flow of force it is necessary to grasp the rules for making the movements continuous, coordinated, and circular. The force in Taiji Quan, which originates from the waist and legs, is applied to the arms and hands, and is focused on the fingers. When the exercises are started, the body moves as an integral whole, with the waist as the pivot. The turn of the waist is in harmony with the stretching and bending of the legs, the outward or inward movement of the feet, and the shift of the body weight. The movement of the arms is also prompted by the turning of the waist.

Stressing the release of force from the waist and legs and the application of integral force does not mean ignoring the role played by the upper limbs. The frequent changes in the movement of the arms in Taiji Quan is an expression of the application of force in concentrated form. For example, when the forearm turns outward, a slight force is applied by its side with the little finger as if twisting the force outward. When the forearm turns inward, a slight force is applied by its side with the thumb as if twisting the force inward. When it is pushed forward, apart from the wrist which slightly resists the force, the middle and index fingers receive the force as if the force is focused on the fingertips in your mind. Although the movements are always changing, the force is applied continuously without interruption.

To sum up, the combination of softness and hardness mentioned above refers to the change of force, and the continuous application of force refers to the integrity of the force.

(III) Concentration and use of the mind to guide the movement.

Taiji Quan calls for the concentration of the mind from beginning to end. After you are skilled in doing the exercises your attention should become focused on the application of force. For example, when you do the stroking exercise, you must have the consciousness of drawing or stroking an object. When you do the pressing exercise, you must have the imagination of pushing and pressing forward. From this related mental activitity guiding the application and change of the force, you can make sure that "once there is an idea, the body moves" and "force is applied as soon as an idea occurs." When these mental activities play a dynamic role in guiding the movements, it not only helps apply the force more fully and make the movements more accurate, but also to produce a direct effect in regulating the central nervous system, strengthening the functions of the organs, and improving the medical effect. Therefore, some people call Taiji Quan an "exercise of consciousness." As to how the mind guides the movements in Taiji Quan, special attention should be paid to the following points in both understanding and practice:

First, concentration of the mind does not mean nervousness and stiff movements. The mental activities must be in harmony with the hardness and softness and the tension and relaxation of the force to form the movements with rhythmic changes. The mental activities and the application of force are two aspects of a unity. They should both reflect the characteristics of "being heavy but not stiff, and being light but not floating."

Second, though the mind, force and movement are identical, there are nevertheless primary and secondary elements.

The mind guides the force, and the force leads to the movements. Taiji Quan calls for "first the mind, and then the body." The force is continuous when the movements change, and the mind is continuous when the force changes. However, relations between the primary and the secondary should not be understood as discontinuity. The changes of mind should be demonstrated in the force and movements. In practicing Taiji Quan, you should not seek "empty quietness" or "the mind with circles and the form without circles." In that case, the mental activities would be unfathomable and incapable of transmission to others.

(IV) Breathing naturally to coordinate the exercises

Breathing should be deep, long, smooth, and natural in Taiji Quan. Beginners should start with natural breathing. After developing some skills, you can consciously guide the breathing on the basis of your own experience and needs to better suit the requirement of the force application and the exercises. Such breathing is called "boxing breathing." For example, when a Taiji exercise is nearing its fixed position, steadiness, compactness and substantial force are called for. At this time, you should consciously coordinate the exercises with breathing so that the chest is relaxed, the ribs restrained, and the belly filled. In this way breathing is used to assist the force. The changes in the Taiji exercises are complicated. Generally speaking, when the movements change from solid to empty, the force is implicit and light, the shoulder blades are unfolded, the chest is expanded, and you should inhale. On the contrary, when the movements change from empty to solid, the force is heavy and concentrated, the shoulder blades are closed, the chest contracts, and you should exhale. Such combinations are identical to physiological needs during the exercises. This is the exact application of the principles of "using the mind to direct the flow of energy and using the energy to motivate the movement of the body" and the "combination of breathing and force." "Boxing breathing" in Taiji Quan is used to change the spontaneous activity of breathing into consciously guided breathing.

The use of "boxing breathing" is by no means absolute since Taiji Quan exercises are not choreographed to the beat of human breathing. Not only do different exercises call for different breathing patterns, but people of differnt physiques doing the same exercise cannot be forced to breathe in the same way. To put it succinctly, "boxing breathing" should be used only when doing the primary exercises or the exercises which clearly call for the opening and closing of the chest and shoulders. When practicing the transitional exercises and exercises which you find difficult to coordinate with breathing, natural breathing or auxiliary breathing (short breathing) is needed for regulation. Therefore, no matter how great your Taiji Quan skills, "boxing breathing" and "natural breathing" are always combined to ensure that breathing and movements are naturally and appropriately coordinated. Don't try listing procedures for breathing, this will make breathing too mechanical and absolute. Ailing or weak people in particular should practice Taiji Quan in the ways suited to their own conditions, using natural and smooth breathing. If they adopt "boxing breathing" in an awkward way, it will harm health instead of improving.

IV. Illustrated Exercises

Notes:

1. In order to clearly describe the exercises, both illustrations and words are used to explain the movements. When doing the exercises, do your best to make the exercises continuous and well connected.

2. In the written description, except for some special remarks, the movement of all parts of the body should be coordinated at the same time, no matter which part of the body is described at any given time. Do not separate them into time sequences.

3. The human body is taken as the standard for the change of direction marking the front, rear, left and right. Imagine that you are facing south when beginning the exercises, this will orient you in the four directions.

4. The lines in the figures indicate the lines passing from one movement to the next and the parts involved. The left hand and the right foot are indicated by dashes (----›) while the right hand and left foot are indicated by a line (—›). The arcs for certain movements are limited by angle and direction and are therefore not described in detail.

5. Certain movements to the back and side are aided by auxiliary figures for comparison. The numbers in brackets are all auxiliary figures.

Names of Exercises

Part I

1. White Crane Spreads Its Wings
2. Brush Knee with Twist Step, Left
3. Single Whip, Left
4. Hand Strums Lute, Left
5. Stroke and Push (Three)
6. Turn to Strike, Parry and Punch, Left

7. Ward off, Stroke, Push and Press, Left

Part II

8. Lean Obliquely
9. Punch Under Elbow
10. Step Back and Whirl Arms on Both Sides (Four)
11. Turn to Push Palms (Four)
12. Hand Strums Lute, Right
13. Brush Knee and Punch Downward

Part III

14. White Snake Sticks out Its Tongue (Two)
15. Pat Foot to Subdue Tiger (Two)
16. Turn Left to Strike
17. Thread Palm with Crouch Stance
18. Fend off on One Leg (Two)
19. Single Whip, Right

Part IV

20. Wave Hands like Clouds, Right (Three)
21. Part Horse's Mane on Both Sides
22. Pat High on Horse
23. Kick with Right Heel
24. Strike Opponent's Ears with Both Fists
25. Kick with Left Heel
26. Strike with Hidden Fist
27. Needle at Sea Bottom
28. Flash Arm

Part V

29. Kick with Right and Left Foot
30. Brush Knee on Left and Right Bow Steps (Two)
31. Step Forward to Strike
32. Apparent Close-Up
33. Wave Hands like Clouds, Left (Three)
34. Turn Right to Strike
35. Work at Shuttles on Both Sides
36. Step Back and Thread Palm

Part VI

37. Press Down Palms with Empty Step
38. Stand on One Leg and Hold out Palm

39. Push Forearm with Horse-Riding Step
40. Turn Body with Big Strokes
41. Swing Palm with Crouch Step
42. Step Forward to Cross Fists
43. Stand on One Leg to Mount Tiger
44. Turn Body for Lotus Kick
45. Draw Bow to Shoot Tiger
46. Turn to Strike, Parry and Punch, Right
47. Ward off, Stroke, Push and Press, Right
48. Cross Hands

Starting Form

(1) Stand erect with feet together, head and neck upright, and chin drawn slightly inward. Relax the chest and abdomen, shoulders and arms down loosely, and hands touching the outer sides of the thighs. Concentrate your mind, look straight ahead and breathe naturally. (Fig. 1)

(2) Move the left foot gently half a step to the left, with the feet shoulder-width apart, toes forward. (Fig. 2)

(3) Raise the arms slowly forward to shoulder level, fingers slightly bent, palms down and elbows slightly dropped. Keep the arms shoulder-width apart. (Fig. 3)

(4) Keep the upper part of the body upright, bend the legs slowly to a half squat, and press the palms gently downward to abdomen level, palms facing the knees. (Figs. 4 (A) and 4 (B))

Points for attention: The height of the bent knees differs from person to person. Generally speaking, the thighs and the floor form an angle of 45 to 60 degrees. Do not let your body rise or fall, but keep roughly the same height throughout the routine, except when you execute certain movements like the crouch step, the standing or squating stance with feet apart, and the standing on one leg.

Part I

1. White Crane Spreads Its Wings

(1) Turn the upper part of the body slightly to the left and shift the body weight onto the left leg. Raise the left palm slightly

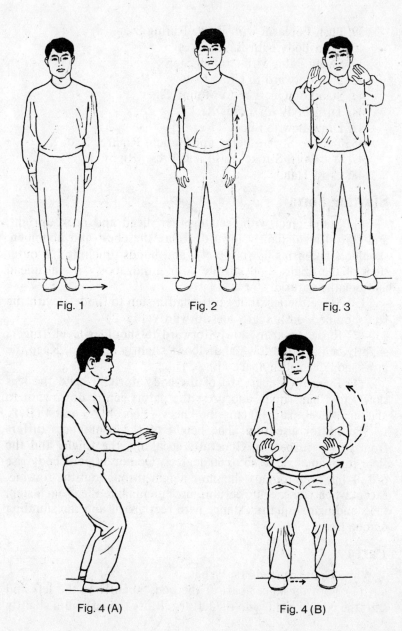

Fig. 1

Fig. 2

Fig. 3

Fig. 4 (A)

Fig. 4 (B)

until the forearm lies across the left part of the chest. Move the right palm to the left in a downward arc past the abdomen until it comes under the left hand, palms facing each other as if holding a ball. At the same time, raise the right foot and place it by the left foot. Look ahead over the left palm. (Fig. 5)

(2) Move the right foot half a step backward to the right, and shift the body weight backward. Turn the waist to the right. Move the right palm from the lower left to the upper right, and the left palm downward past the right shouldler in arcs. Look at the right palm. (Fig. 6)

(3) Turn the upper part of the body slightly to the left and face the front. Move the palms in arcs in opposite directions, press the left hand on the left hip, palm down and fingers pointing forward, and raise the right hand to the upper right before the forehead, palm inward, and both arms curved. At the same time, move the left foot slightly inward, ball of foot on the floor and knee slightly bent to form a left empty step. Look straight ahead. (Fig. 7)

Points for attention: In executing the empty step, the feet form an angle of about 45 degrees. Keep the knee of the rear leg over the toes and the buttock over the heel. Keep the upper part of the body upright and pull the buttocks in. Do not turn the knees inward or outward too much.

2. Brush Knee with Twist Step, Left

(1) Turn the upper part of the body slightly to the left, and move the right hand in an arc downward past the front of the body, and the left hand in an arc upward past the side of the body. (Fig. 8)

(2) Turn the upper part of the body to the right, move the right hand in an arc from below to the upper right backward to ear level, palm obliquely up, and at the same time, move the left hand in an arc from before the body to the lower right to before the right part of the chest, palm obliquely down. At the same time, move the left foot back to the inner side of the right foot. Look at the right palm. (Fig. 9)

(3) Turn the upper part of the body slightly to the left, move the left foot one step forward to the left with the feet about 30

Fig. 5

Fig. 6

Fig. 7

Fig. 8

centimetres apart, and shift the body weight forward, left leg bent and right leg straightened to form a left bow step. At the same time, pull the right hand back past the right ear and push it forward, fingers to nose level. Move the left hand downward to the left around the left knee and press it by the left hip, palm down and fingers pointing forward. Keep the upper part of the body upright and relax the waist and hips. Look at the right hand. (Fig. 10)

Points for attention: In executing the bow step, the feet form an angle of about 45 to 60 degrees (when necessary, readjust the heel of the rear foot by moving it backward). The left knee and the left toes form a perpendicular line. In order to keep balanced, do not put both feet on the same line, or cross them. Keep the feet 10 to 30 centimetres apart horizontally, depending on the degree of the turn of the body and the direction for the force applied.

3. Single Whip, Left

(1) Sit back and shift the weight onto the right leg, toes of

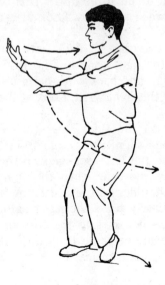 

Fig. 9   Fig. 10

the left foot raised and turned slightly inward, while turning the upper part of the body to the right. Move the right arm backward to the right, palm down, and move the left hand to the front of the body in an arc from the lower left side to shoulder level, palm obliquely down. The head follows the body's turn. Look ahead. (Fig. 11)

(2) Land the left foot firmly on the floor, shift the weight to the left leg and withdraw the right foot to the inner side of the left foot. At the same time, move the left forearm slightly back and turn the right arm outward, palm up, and thread it forward to the left under the left elbow. (Fig. 12)

(3) Move the right foot one step forward to the right (imagine facing south when starting the exercises, and in this exercise you should now be facing west). Keep the feet about 10 centimetres apart horizontally. Shift the weight forward to form the right bow step. At the same time, place the left palm by the inner side of the right wrist (the same side as the palm). Move both hands from the left forward in a horizontal semicircle, right palm obliquely inward and left palm obliquely outward. Turn the upper part of the body to the front, and relax the waist and hips. Look at the front palm. (Fig. 13)

(4) Continue from the previous exercise. Sit back with the toes of the right tiptoes raised. Move the right hand in a horizontal semicircle from the front to the right and backward, palm up, with the left palm on the inner side of the right wrist. Look at the front hand. (Fig. 14)

(5) Land the right foot firmly on the floor, toes turned inward, turn the upper part of the body slightly to the left, shift the weight to the right leg, and move the left foot back to the inner side of the right foot. At the same time, turn the right forearm inward in front of the right shoulder before stretching it forward in a curve, and then immediately press the right palm and change it into a hook hand when it comes to the forward right. Turn the left forearm outward at the same time until it stops at the inner side of the right ribs, palm inside. Look at the right hand. (Fig. 15)

(6) Turn the upper part of the body slightly to the left, move

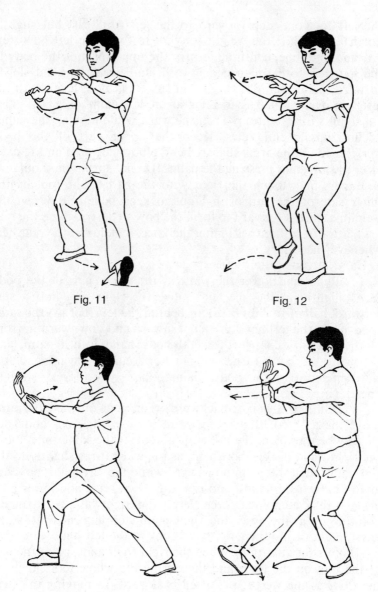

Fig. 11

Fig. 12

Fig. 13

Fig. 14

the left foot one step forward to the left (due east but slightly north) , and shift the weight forward to form the left bow step. At the same time, continue to turn the upper part of the body to the left, left forearm turned inward, and push the hand slowly forward, palm facing forward and fingers at nose level, with the left arm over the left foot. Look at the left palm. (Fig. 16)

Points for attention: Turn the waist while moving the hands in horizontal semicircles. Keep the upper part of the body upright. Keep the arms slightly bent, elbows lowered and relaxed after pushing and pressing the palms. Do not shrug the shoulders. Beginners may touch the floor with the ball of the foot by the inner side of the supporting foot to keep balanced. When the weight is shifted forward to form the bow step, straighten the rear leg naturally without stiffening the knee, and adjust the rear heel whenever necessary.

4. Hand Strums Lute, Left

1. Relax and lower the waist as the upper part of the body turns slightly to the left, and move the right foot half a step forward, ball of foot on the floor behind the left foot. At the same time, move the left hand in an arc inward and downward in front of the left hip, change the right hook hand into a palm, and following the body turn, swing it horizontally inward and forward in front of the body, palm obliquely up. Look straight ahead. (Fig. 17)

(2) Shift the weight backward, right foot on the floor, and move the left foot slightly forward, heel on the floor and knee slightly bent to form the left empty step. At the same time, move the right hand back, elbow bent, as the waist turns slightly to the right, and turn the palm downward while the left hand moves in an arc outward, forward and upward. Then relax and lower both arms with a combined force, left palm rightward with fingers pointing up at the nose, and right palm stopping in front of the chest, palm facing the left elbow. Look at the left hand. (Fig. 18)

Points for attention: When the right foot lands, place the ball of the foot on the floor and then bring the whole foot slowly to the floor as the weight is shifted backward. In moving the step, raise the heel first and then the whole foot gently. Apply the force

Fig. 15

Fig. 16

Fig. 17

Fig. 18

gently and evenly when landing or raising the feet. Do not stamp or hammer the floor suddenly.

5. Stroke and Push

(1) Move the left foot slightly outward to the left and then place it fully on the floor with the weight shifted forward to form the left bow step. Turn the upper part of the body slightly to the right. Thread the right hand forward over the left forearm and move it in an arc from left to forward right horizontally, palm obliquely down. Turn the left hand slightly outward (palm obliquely up), and move it in an arc backward to under the inner side of the right elbow. Look at the right hand. (Figs. 19-20)

(2) Pull both palms downward as if stroking a long beard, left palm to the outer side of the left hip and right palm in front of the abdomen. At the same time, move the right foot backward to the inner side of the left foot. Look ahead to the right. (Fig. 21)

(3) Move the right foot one step forward to the right (southeast), heel on the floor. At the same time, turn both forearms (left arm inward and right arm outward), turn both palms over and raise them to chest level, arms bent and palms facing each other. Turn the head with the body naturally. (Fig. 22)

(4) Land the right foot firmly on the floor and shift the weight forward to form the right bow step. Push both arms forward, arms forming a circle, left fingers close to the right wrist, and left palm outward with fingers obliquely up and right palm inward with fingers leftward at shoulder level. Look at the right wrist. This is the right stroking and pushing exercise. (Fig. 23)

(5) Shift the weight backward, toes of the right foot raised and turned slightly inward, and then place them on the floor to form the right bow step. At the same time, turn the upper part of the body to the left, thread the left hand forward above the right forearm and move it horizontally forward in an arc, and move the right palm slightly backward in an arc to under the inner side of the left elbow. Look at the left palm. (Figs. 24-25)

(6) The left stroking and pushing exercise is the same as the right stroking and pushing exercise, only in a different direction

Fig. 19

Fig. 20

Fig. 21

Fig. 22

Fig. 23

Fig. 24

Fig. 25

Fig. 26

(northeast). (Figs. 26-28)

(7) Repeat the movements in (1) to (4). (Figs. 29-33)

Points for attention: From stroking to pushing, raise both palms while turning them in front of the body within the limits of a shoulder-width. Stroking should be coordinated with the withdrawing of the foot, and pushing with the bending of the leg. In withdrawing the foot, the beginner may rest the ball on the floor by the inner side of the supporting foot before stepping forward in order to keep balance. This is permitted in similar movements throughout the routine.

6. Turn to Strike, Parry and Punch, Left

(1) Shift the weight backward, toes of the right foot outward, and turn the upper part of the body to the right. Move the left hand forward to the left (due east), palm obliquely down, and move the right hand in an arc downward at the same time, palm up. (Fig. 34)

(2) Shift the weight forward, and move the left foot to the inner side of the right foot. Move the right hand in an arc from

Fig. 27   Fig. 28

Fig. 29

Fig. 30

Fig. 31

Fig. 32

Fig. 33   Fig. 34

below to the right backward, and then upward to the front at shoulder level, palm down. Change the left palm into a fist, and move it downward in an arc to the right part of the chest, knuckles up. Look straight ahead. (Fig. 35)

(3) Take a skip forward with the left foot, heel on the floor and toes outward. Strike forward with the left fist (due east) to chest level, knuckles down. Move the right hand past the outer side of the left forearm and press it by the side of the right hip. Look at the left fist. (Fig. 36)

(4) Shift the weight forward, land the left foot on the floor, and move the right foot past the inner side of the left foot to step forward while turning the waist to the left. Move the left fist in an arc to the left side of the waist, knuckles down. Move the right hand forward in an arc past the right side of the body for a parry at chest level, palm forward down. Look at the right palm. (Fig. 37)

(5) Shift the weight forward to form the right bow step and punch forward with the left fist, knuckles upward at chest level.

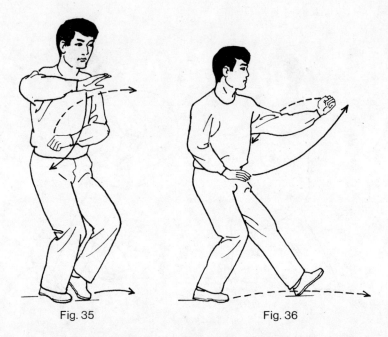

Fig. 35   Fig. 36

Move the right palm back to the inner side of the left forearm at the same time. Look at the left fist. (Fig. 38)

Points for attention: The two vertical arcs should be symmetrical. While withdrawing the left fist after striking, turn the left forearm inward first and then outward. When parrying with the right palm, turn the right forearm outward first and then inward.

7. Ward off, Stroke, Push and Press, Left

(1) Sit back, toes of the right foot outward, and turn the waist to the right. Turn the right forearm outward, and move the right hand in an arc downward, palm up. Change the left fist into a palm, and turn the forearm inward to push it forward, palm turned downward. (Fig. 39)

(2) Land the right foot, shift the weight forward, and withdraw the left foot to the inner side of the right foot. At the same time, move the left hand downward to in front of the waist and the right hand backward and upward to in front of the chest, both in arcs, palms facing each other as if holding a ball. (Fig. 40)

(3) Turn the upper part of the body slightly to the left, move

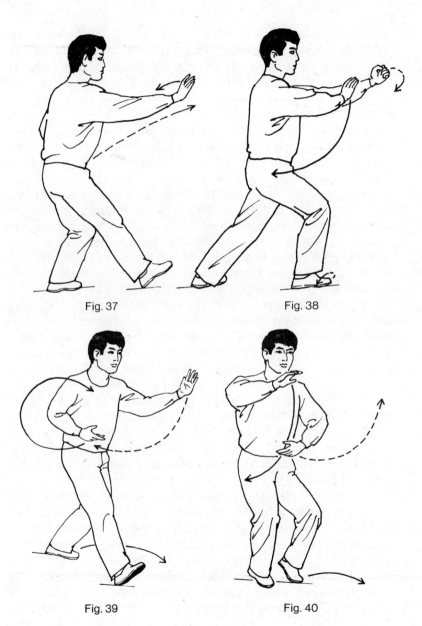

Fig. 37

Fig. 38

Fig. 39

Fig. 40

the left foot one step forward, shift the weight forward, and straighten the rear leg, heel backward, to form the left bow step. At the same time, move the left forearm forward, elbow slightly bent, to shoulder level, palm inward, as if to ward off a blow, while the right palm is pressed downward to the right hip. Look at the left forearm. (Fig. 41)

(4) Turn the waist slightly to the left, move the left hand forward and turn it over, palm down, while the right forearm is turned outward, palm up, and is moved upward and forward past the abdomen to under the left forearm. (Fig. 42)

(5) Turn the upper part of the body to the right, pull both hands downward past the abdomen as if stroking a long beard, and then move them upward and backward in an arc to the right until the right hand reaches shoulder level, palm obliquely up, and the left forearm is bent in front of the chest, palm obliquely inward. At the same time, sit back and bend the right leg with the weight almost on it. Look at the right palm. (Fig. 43)

(6) Turn the upper part of the body to the left, face forward, and shift the weight forward to form the left bow step. Bend the right arm at the elbow, and move the hand back, palm fingers close to the wrist of the left hand. Push both hands forward slowly at shoulder level, left palm inward and right palm forward, and form arms into a semicircle. Look at the left wrist. (Fig. 44)

(7) Push the right palm forward over the left wrist, and separate the hands until they are a shoulder-width apart, palms down. Sit back immediately, and shift the weight onto the right leg, left toes up. Bend both arms at the elbow, and withdraw them to in front of the chest, palms obliquely down. Look straight ahead. (Fig. 45)

(8) Bend the left leg forward to form the left bow step. Move both palms downward past the abdomen to press them forward and upward with the wrist at shoulder level. Relax the waist and hips, drop the shoulders and elbows, and keep the wrists and palms at ease. Look straight ahead. (Fig. 46)

Points for attention: From stroking to pushing, move the hands backward. From pushing to pressing, be sure to draw the buttocks in, and keep the upper part of the body upright, not

Fig. 41

Fig. 42

Fig. 43

Fig. 44

Fig. 45   Fig. 46

leading forward or backward.

Part II

8. Lean Obliquely

(1) Shift the weight to the right leg, toes of the left foot inward, and turn the body to the right. Move the right hand in an arc to the right side of the body and the left hand in an arc symmetrically to the left side of the body, both elbows slightly bent and palms forward. Look at the right hand. (Fig. 47)

(2) Shift the weight to the left leg and withdraw the right foot to the inner side of the left foot. At the same time, move the right hand in an arc downward and leftward, and then back to the front of the chest at shoulder level, and the left hand back until they cross at the wrists obliquely, both palms inward (right hand outside). Look forward. (Fig. 48)

(3) Turn the upper part of the body slightly to the right, and move the right foot forward to the right (due west 30° by north), heel on the floor. Turn the front forearm slightly inward, both

Fig. 47   Fig. 48

hands clenched in fists. Look ahead. (Fig. 49)

(4) Shift the weight forward and straighten the left leg naturally (heel backward) to form the right bow step. At the same time, separate the hands, and move the left downward to the left hip, knuckles obliquely forward, and the right upward in front of the forehead, knuckles inward. Lean the upper part of the body obliquely southwestward. Look ahead to the left. (Fig. 50)

Points for attention: In the fixed position, the bow step faces west by north and the upper part of the body turns to the west by south. Drop the shoulders and relax the hips. Extend the shoulders and arms slightly outward. Do not lean sideways.

9. Punch Under Elbow

(1) Shift the weight leftward, toes of the right foot raised and turned inward, and turn the upper part of the body to the left. Change the right fist into a palm and turn it up in an inward arc. At the same time, change the left fist into a palm and turn it down in an inward arc. Look at the right palm. (Fig. 51)

(2) Shift the weight rightward and move the left foot back to

Fig. 49

Fig. 50

the inner side of the right foot. Turn the right palm down and bend the arm in front of the right part of the chest, and turn the left palm up and move it in an arc past the abdomen to the right to face the right palm as if holding a ball. Look at the right palm. (Fig. 52)

(3) Turn the upper part of the body to the left, and skip the left foot forward to the left, heel on the floor and toes up and outward. Move the left palm from under the right forearm in an arc to the upper left, palm inward at nose level, and the right palm in an arc past the chest downward to the right of the hip. Look at the left palm. (Fig. 53)

(4) Continue to turn the upper part of the body to the left, land the left foot on the floor, shift the weight forward to the left leg, and move the right foot half a step forward, ball on the floor behind the left foot. Turn the left forearm down and move the left palm in an arc to the left and downward to the side of the body, and the right palm to the right and forward to in front of the body, palm obliquely up to nose level. Face due east and look

Fig. 51

Fig. 52

Fig. 53

Fig. 54

ahead. (Fig. 54)

(5) Shift the weight backward, land the right foot on the floor, and move the left foot slightly forward, heel on the floor to form the left empty step. Thread the left palm forward from above the right wrist, palm to the right and fingers pointing to the nose. At the same time, change the right palm into a fist and move it back to under the inner side of the left elbow, knuckles up. Look at the left palm. (Fig. 55)

Points for attention: The whole exercise should be done in a continuous flow. Use the waist as the axis to motivate the limbs. In the fixed position, relax the shoulders and drop the elbows slightly, with the right fist under the left elbow to the right. Keep the chest relaxed.

10. Step Back and Whirl Arms on Both Sides (Four)

(1) Turn the upper part of the body to the right, and change the right fist into a palm, palm up, and move it in a curve past the right hip backward and raise it horizontally to the shoulder level, elbow slightly bent. At the same time, turn the left arm outward, palm up, and raise the left foot gently. The eyes first turn to the right as the body turns, and then turn to the left palm. (Fig. 56)

(2) Raise the left foot a bit, toes down, and step backward, ball of foot on the floor. Shift the weight backward, and land the left foot on the floor, the heel of the right foot slightly outward and toes forward to form the right empty step. At the same time, bend the right arm at the elbow, move the right palm back past the right ear and push it forward, palm forward at shoulder level. Withdraw the left hand downward to before the left hip. Look at the right palm. Keep the upper part of the body upright, and relax the waist and hips. (Fig. 57)

(3) Turn the upper part of the body to the left, and move the left palm downward and to the left backward in an arc and raise it horizontally, palm up. At the same time, turn the right arm outward, palm up. Look to the left first as the body turns, and then to the right palm. (Fig. 58)

(4) Raise the right foot gently and move it backward, ball first on the floor and then the whole foot. Shift the weight to the

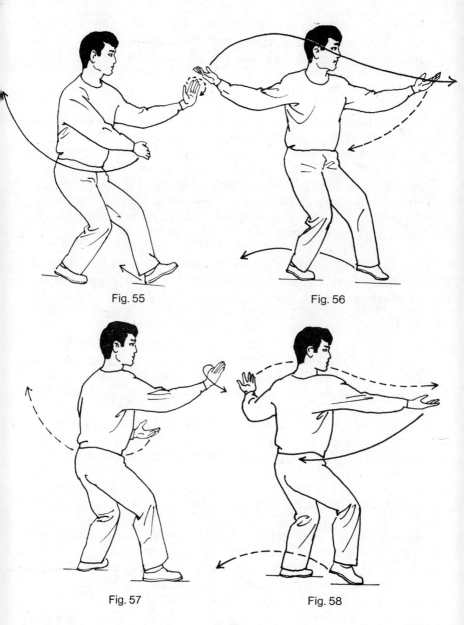

Fig. 55

Fig. 56

Fig. 57

Fig. 58

right leg, heel of the left foot slightly outward. Bend the left knee slightly to form the left empty step. Bend the left arm at elbow, and move the palm past the left ear to push forward, palm forward at shoulder level. Move the right palm downward and backward to in front of the right hip. Look at the left palm. (Fig. 59)

(5) Repeat the movements from (1) to (4) once each on the left and right sides. (Figs. 60-63)

Points for attention: In moving the foot backward, land the ball first on the floor, and then the whole foot. Shift the weight backward to make a clear distinction between the empty and the solid when changing steps. At the same time, keep the feet about 10 centimetres apart. To remain balanced, do not cross the legs when stepping backward.

11. Turn to Push Palms (Four)

(1) Withdraw the left foot to behind the right foot, ball on the floor. Turn the left palm outward and move it first upward and then downward to in front of the right side of the chest, palm down. Move the right palm in a curve upward to the right, palm up at head level. Look at the right palm. (Fig. 64)

(2) Pivot on the ball of the left foot and the right heel to turn the body to the left backward, and keep the weight on the right leg after the turn. Bend the right arm, move the palm back, and press the left hand slightly downward. Look ahead to the left (northwest). (Fig. 65)

(3) Move the left foot one step forward (northwest), with the right foot following immediately to land behind the left foot, ball touching the floor to form the T-shaped step. At the same time, move the left palm downward to circle around the left knee and press it to the left side of the hip, palm forward and fingers up to nose level. Look at the right palm. (Fig. 66)

(4) Pivot on the left heel and ball of the right foot to turn the body to the right backward, and keep the weight on the left leg after the turn. At the same time, turn the left arm outward and move it to the left and upward in an arc to head level, palm up. Move the right palm down to in front of the left side of the chest, palm down. Look forward to the right. (Fig. 67)

Fig. 59

Fig. 60

Fig. 61

Fig. 62

Fig. 63

Fig. 64

Fig. 65

Fig. 66

(5) Move the right foot forward (southeast) with the left foot immediately following half a step behind the right foot to form the T-shaped step. Circle the right palm around the right knee, palm fingers forward, and press it by the right hip. Push the left palm forward past the ear, palm forward and fingers up to nose level. Look at the left palm. (Fig. 68)

(6) Repeat the movements for turning the body to push palms once on each side. The movements are exactly the same, but the directions should be northeast and southwest, just opposite of the two previous exercises. (Figs. 69-72)

Points for attention: In executing the T-shaped step, keep the feet about 10 centimetres apart for easier turning. In turning the body, keep the weight between the feet, and after turning, shift the weight to the rear leg to make the turning easy. The whole exercise should be done with both ease and steadiness.

12. Hand Strums Lute, Right

(1) Move the left foot half a step backward (slightly to the left) and shift the weight to the left leg. Turn the upper part of

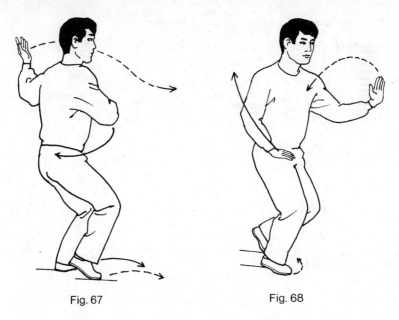

Fig. 67   Fig. 68

49

Fig. 69

Fig. 70

Fig. 71

Fig. 72

the body to the left. Bend the left arm and move it back with the palm in front of the left side of the chest, palm obliquely down. Move the right palm in an arc forward and upward to in front of the body, palm obliquely to the left. The head follows the body turn. Look ahead. (Fig. 73)

(2) Turn the upper part of the body slightly to the right, lower the right palm slightly, forearm slightly turned outward and palm to the left and fingers pointing to the nose. Move the left palm forward past the left side of the chest to the inner side of the right arm, palm to the right to face right elbow. At the same time, raise the right foot slightly, heel on the floor and knee slightly bent to form the right empty step. Face due west and look at the right palm. (Fig. 74)

Points for attention: In the fixed position, close the arms gently. Keep the head and the upper part of the body upright, and neck erect. Drop the shoulders, relax the waist, and face due west.

13. Brush Knee and Punch Downward

(1) Turn the upper body to the left, and move the right foot

Fig. 73

Fig. 74

ahead of the left foot, toes on the floor. Pull both hands downward to in front of the abdomen, palms obliquely facing each other. The head follows the body turn. Look ahead. (Fig. 75)

(2) Move the right foot half a step forward, shift the weight forward to the right leg with the left foot following behind the right foot, ball of foot on the floor. Turn both hands over in front of the chest and at the same time move them in an arc to the left and forward, right palm up to shoulder level and left palm down on the inner side of the wrist of the right hand. Look at the right palm. (Figs. 76-77)

(3) Shift the weight to the left leg, turn the upper part of the body to the left, turn up the left forearm and move it downward, backward and then upward to head level. Move the right palm in an arc to the left and press it in front of the left side of the chest, palm down. Look at the left palm. (Fig. 78)

(4) Turn the upper part of the body to the right, move the right foot forward and straighten the left leg to form the right bow step. Circle the right palm around the right knee and press it by the right hip, fingers pointing forward. Change the left palm into a fist and strike forward past the ear and downward to abdomenal level, knuckles forward. Look forward down. (Fig. 79)

Points for attention: Move the arms alternately, one in a vertical arc and the other in a horizontal arc. The movements should be well coordinated. Use the waist to guide the movements. In the fixed position, do not lean the upper part of the body forward too much. The stance is a twist step. In all twist-shaped steps, be sure to keep the feet apart for balance. Keep the upper part of the body natural.

Part III

14. White Snake Sticks Out Its Tongue (Two)

(1) Shift the weight backward, toes of the right foot raised. Move the left fist up and hold the right palm up. Look at the right fist. (Fig. 80)

(2) Turn the right foot inward, turn the body to the left backward and shift the weight to the right. Raise the left foot to turn outward. Pivoting on the toes of the right foot, turn the body to cross

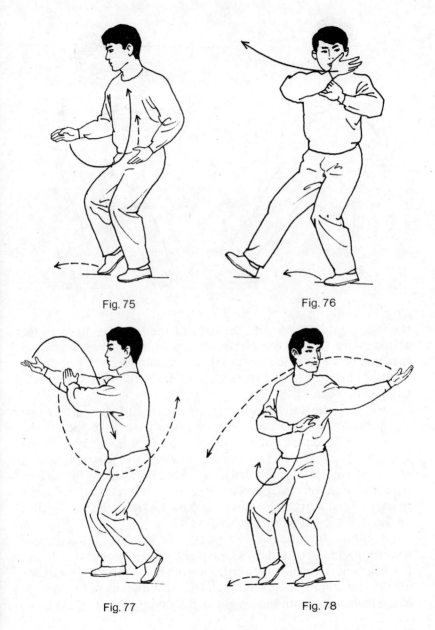

Fig. 75

Fig. 76

Fig. 77

Fig. 78

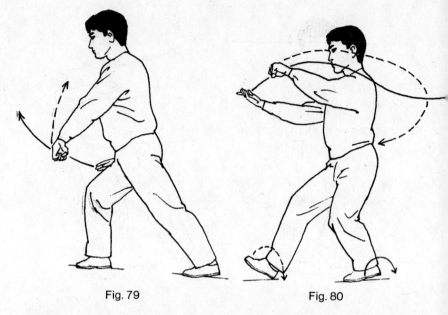

Fig. 79   Fig. 80

the legs, right knee close to the back of the left knee to form the seated stance. Change the left fist into a palm and move it down past the front of the body to the waist, palm up, and push the right palm forward past the ear to chest level, palm forward. Look at the right palm. (Fig. 81)

(3) Shift the weight forward, raise the right foot and take one step forward, toes outward. Turn the upper part of the body to the right. Pivoting on the ball of the left foot, turn the body with the left heel lifted off the floor to cross the legs and form the seated stance. Move the left palm backward and upward past the side of the ear to push forward, palm forward at chest level. Turn the right palm over and move it downward and backward to the waist, palm up. Look at the left palm. (Figs. 82-83)

Points for attention: When moving the left foot outward, raise it at the original spot and then land it sideways in front of the body. In turning and stepping forward, keep the body upright. In executing the seated stance, squat on both legs, rear knee close to the back of the front knee, with the weight slightly on the front leg.

Fig. 81   Fig. 82

15. Pat Foot to Subdue Tiger (Two)

(1) Shift the weight forward and skip the left foot forward. Move the left palm in an arc to the lower left and the right palm in an arc backward and upward to the right side of the head, ready to pat the foot. Look straight ahead. (Fig. 84)

(2) Land the left foot, stand on the left leg, and kick forward and upward with the right foot, instep naturally flat. Pat the instep with the right palm, and move the left palm in an arc backward and upward to the left behind, palm outward at shoulder level. Look at the front palm. (Fig. 85)

(3) Land the right foot to the left in front of the left foot and raise the left foot as soon as the right foot lands. At the same time, move both palms horizontally to the right, palms down. Look at the right palm. (Fig. 86)

(4) Land the left foot forward to the left (due north), and straighten the right leg to form the left bow step (northward). Move both palms in arcs past the abdomen downward to the left as the body turns to the left. Clench the hands into fists while

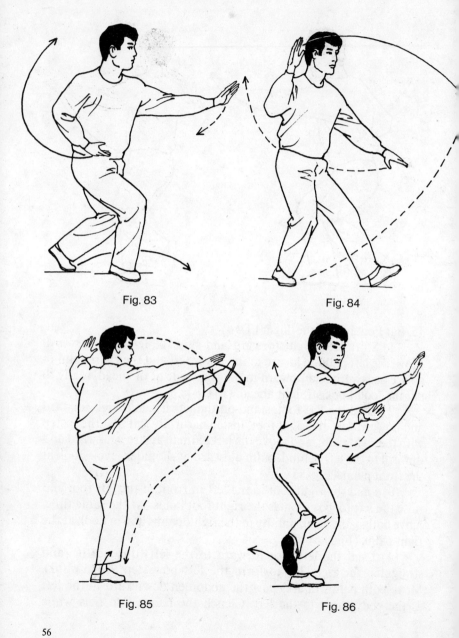

Fig. 83

Fig. 84

Fig. 85

Fig. 86

drawing the arcs. Look at the left fist. (Fig. 87)

(5) Continue from the previous movement. Sweep the left fist to the right horizontally, bent at the elbow, to in front of the forehead, knuckles obliquely outward. Sweep the right fist to the left horizontally to in front of the left ribs, knuckles obliquely up. Keep the waist and hips relaxed. Turn the eyes ahead and to the right (due east). (Fig. 88)

(6) Shift the weight backward, toes of the left foot turned inward as the upper part of the body turns to the right. At the same time, change both fists into palms, move the left hand back in front of the chest, palm obliquely up, and thrust the right hand forward over the left forearm, palm obliquely down. Look straight ahead. (Fig. 89)

(7) Land the left foot, shift the weight to the left leg, and skip the right foot forward (due east) past the inner side of the left foot. Move the left hand in a vertical semicircle downward, backward and upward to the left side of the head, palm forward, ready to pat the foot. Move the right palm forward and downward to draw a vertical semicircle to the side of the right hip. Look straight ahead. (Figs. 90-91)

(8) Stand on the right leg, and kick forward and upward with the left foot, instep flat. Pat the instep with the left palm while moving the right palm backward and upward to draw an arc to the right behind at shoulder level, palm outward. Look at the left palm. (Fig. 92)

(9) Land the left foot to the right in front of the right foot, and raise the right foot as soon as the left foot lands. At the same time, swing both palms horizontally to the left, palms down. Look at the left palm. (Fig. 93)

(10) Land the right foot to the right (due south), and bend the right leg to form the right bow step (southward). Move both palms in arcs downward to the right past the abdomen, and gradually clench the hands into fists. Look at the right fist. (Fig. 94)

(11) Continue from the previous movement. Sweep the right fist horizontally to the left, bent at the elbow, to in front of the right side of the forehead, knuckles obliquely outward. Sweep the

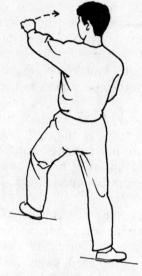

Fig. 87

Fig. 88 (A)

Fig. 88 (B)

Fig. 89

Fig. 90

Fig. 91

Fig. 92

Fig. 93

left fist horizontally to the right in front of the right ribs, knuckles obliquely upward. Keep the waist and hips relaxed. Turn the eyes ahead and to the left (due east). (Fig. 95)

Points for attention: Before patting the foot, the movements of the arms should be well coordinated with the steps. Do not thrust the chest out or straighten the arms. While patting the foot, stand firmly on the supporting leg, slightly bent. The height for patting the foot differs from person to person. Don't bend forward or hold your breath in order to reach the height. After patting the foot, move the shank back before landing. The landing should be light-footed and slow. Do not jump high or too far. Drop the foot gently on the floor near the supporting leg. After patting, you may also drop the foot behind the supporting leg and immediately move the foot backward and turn your body to do the subduing-the-tiger exercise. Drop the foot gently and move it smoothly and steadily when executing the back cross step.

16. Turn Left to Strike

(1) Shift the weight backward, right foot turned inward, and

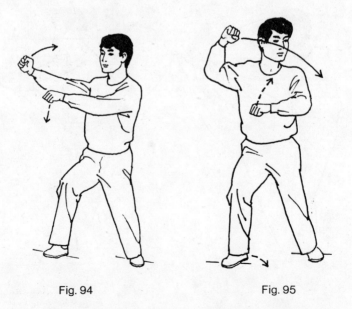

Fig. 94   Fig. 95

turn the upper part of the body to the left. At the same time, change the right fist into a palm, palm obliquely up, and move it to in front of the chest. Change the left fist into a palm too, palm obliquely down, and thrust it forward over the right forearm. Look ahead. (Fig. 96)

(2) Land the right foot firmly on the floor, and shift the weight to the right leg. Move the left palm in an arc slightly upward and forward, palm down, and the right palm in an arc downward and backward to in front of the right hip, palm up. Look at the left palm. (Fig. 97)

(3) Turn the upper part of the body to the right, and move the left foot to the inner side of the right foot. Move the left hand downward, clench it into a fist, and place it in front of the abdomen, knuckles obliquely outward. Move the right palm in an arc backward and upward and then in front of the body, and turn the palm downward and place it on the inner side of the left forearm (on the same side as the palm). Look ahead and to the left. (Fig. 98)

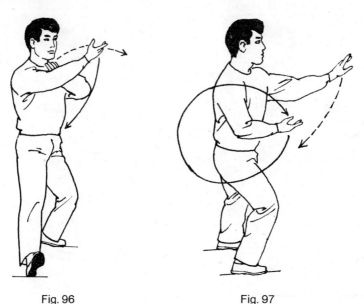

Fig. 96   Fig. 97

(4) Turn the upper part of the body slightly to the left, move the left foot one step forward to the left (northeast), and shift the weight forward to form the left bow step. Raise the left fist and strike forward to head level, knuckles obliquely down, and keep the right palm on the innèr side of the left forearm. (Fig. 99)

Points for attention: Before striking, do not turn the right foot inward too much, and the left palm should be thrust forward due east. While moving the hands back, cross them to draw circles. Clench the left hand into a fist while pulling it back, but not in the stroking form. The turning of the waist and all movements of the body should be well coordinated throughout the exercise.

17. Thread Fists with Crouch Stance

(1) Shift the weight backward, toes of the left foot raised and turned slightly outward, and turn the upper part of the body slightly to the left. Change the left fist into a palm and move it in an arc upward and to the left, and the right palm in an arc downward and to the right, both palms down. (Fig. 100)

Fig. 98   Fig. 99

(2) Continue from the previous movement, land the left foot firmly on the floor, shift the weight forward, and place the right foot to the inner side of the left foot. Continue to move both palms in vertical circles and at the same time clench them into fists, knuckles of the left hand outward in front of the abdomen and those of the right hand outward in front of the eyes. Look straight ahead. (Fig. 101)

(3) Drop the right arm, elbow bent, and thread the left fist upward outside the right forearm. At the same time, bend the left leg to the squating position and stretch the right foot forward to the right side (due east by south about 30 degrees) to form the right crouch stance. Look ahead and to the right. (Fig. 102)

(4) Turn the upper part of the body to the right, thread the right fist forward to the right past the abdomen along the inner side of the right leg, and extend the left fist backward to the upper left, knuckles of both hands backward. Look at the right fist. (Fig. 103)

Points for attention: Do not turn the toes of the left foot

Fig. 100

Fig. 101

Fig. 102   Fig. 103

outward too much. Touch the floor for a pause after moving the right foot by the left foot. In executing the crouch stance, first bend the left leg and then immediately extend the right leg to the right side (do not slip the heel of the right foot along the floor). Then turn the body to thread the fists. Place both feet firmly on the floor. Do not raise the heels. Elderly people may squat halfway by bending the left leg in a semi-crouching stance.

18. Fend Off on One Leg (Two)

(1) Shift the weight forward, toes of the right foot turned outward and toes of the left foot turned inward. Straighten the left leg slightly. At the same time, raise the right fist slightly and lower the left fist slightly, knuckles of both hands upward. Look ahead. (Fig. 104)

(2) Keep the right foot on the floor and raise the left foot. Change the right fist into a palm and turn it slightly inward, and change the left fist into a palm, lower it to the side of the waist side and thread it forward and upward, palm inward. Look ahead. (Fig. 105)

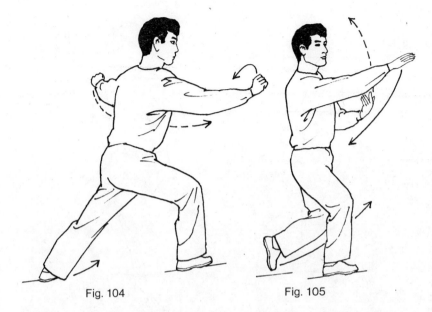

Fig. 104   Fig. 105

(3) Stand firmly on the right leg, slightly bent, and bend the left leg in front, instep flat. Press the right palm in front of the right hip, fingers pointing leftward, and thread the left palm over the inner side of the right forearm and turn the palm over in front of the head, fingers pointing to the right and palm obliquely up. Look ahead. (Fig. 106)

(4) Land the left foot forward (slightly to the left), shift the weight forward, stand on the left leg, and raise the right leg to the front of the body, instep flat. Turn the right forearm outward, palm inward, thread it upward past the inner side of the left forearm, and turn the palm over so that it stops above and in front of the head (fingers pointing to the left and palm obliquely up). Drop the left palm and press it to the front of the left hip (fingers pointing to the right). Look ahead. (Figs. 107-109)

Points for attention: While standing on one leg, the supporting leg should be slightly bent, and the knee should not be stiff and straight. Turn the waist gently while the right palm is lifted upward. When the palm is propped up above the head, keep the

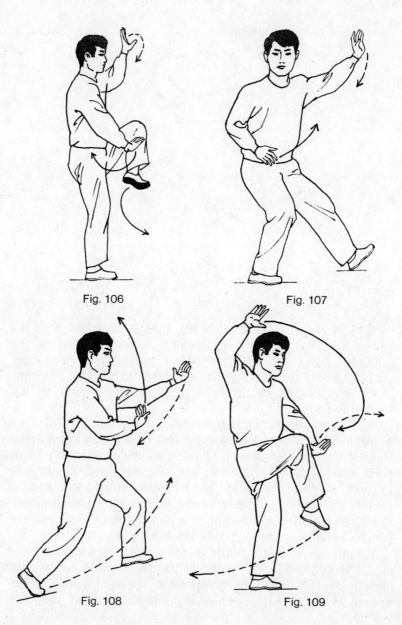

Fig. 106

Fig. 107

Fig. 108

Fig. 109

upper part of the body upright, raise the head upward and relax the whole body.

19. Single Whip, Right

(1) Move the right foot one step backward and bend the left leg to form the left bow step. At the same time, lower the right palm forward and downward, palm up, and extend the left palm upward and forward over the right forearm, palm down. Look at the left palm. (Fig. 110)

(2) Shift the weight backward and pull both palms downward and backward together in front of the abdomen. The head follows the body's turn. (Fig. 111)

(3) Turn the left palm over while moving it upward past the abdomen to chest level, palm inward, and at the same time turn the right palm over and raise it, palm forward and fingers on the inner side of the left wrist. (Fig. 112)

(4) Shift the weight forward, bend the left leg forward, and turn the upper part of the body to the left. Move the left palm forward in a horizontal circle from the right to shoulder level, palm obliquely inward and fingers of the right palm on the inner side of the left wrist. The eyes follow the movement of the left palm. (Fig. 113)

(5) Shift the weight backward, toes of the left foot raised. Bend the left arm at the elbow and move the palm in a horizontal circle to the left and backward, palm up while the right palm turns. Look at the left palm. (Fig. 114)

(6) Turn the toes of the left foot inward and keep the whole foot on the floor, weight shifted to the left leg. Press the left palm forward to the left as the left forearm is turned inward, and immediately change it into a hook. Turn the right forearm slightly outward, palm inward and place it at the bend of the elbow. At the same time, move the right foot back to the inner side of the left foot. Look at the left hook hand. (Fig. 115)

(7) Turn the upper part of the body slightly to the right, and move the right foot forward to the right (due west slightly by north), weight shifted forward to form the right bow step. Turn the right palm over slowly as the body turns and push it forward, fingers up to nose level and palm forward, right elbow facing the

Fig. 110

Fig. 111

Fig. 112

Fig. 113

Fig. 114   Fig. 115

right knee. Look at the right palm. (Fig. 116)

Points for attention: The bow step should be executed slightly to the northwest. Keep the chest drawn in and the elbows and shoulders relaxed. Do not stiffen the arms. They should not be fully extended to form a straight line. Push the palm in an arc while it is turned over and in coordination with the turning of the waist. Relax the shoulders and wrists when the exercise nears the end.

Part IV

20. Wave Hands like Clouds, Right (Three)

(1) Turn the upper part of the body to the left and shift the weight to the left leg, toes of the right foot inward. Move the right palm in a vertical circle downward and in front of the left shoulder, palm inward. Look at the left hook hand. (Fig. 117)

(2) The right palm continues to draw a vertical cycle to the right, palm inward. Change the left hook into a palm and move it in a vertical circle downward past the abdomen. At the same

Fig. 116   Fig. 117

time, turn the left forearm outward, palm gradually from outward to inward, and shift the weight gradually to the right leg.
Both the upper part of the body and the eyes follow the right
palm. (Figs. 118-119)

(3) Continue to turn the upper part of the body to the right.
Move the right palm to the right side of the body, forearm turned
inward and palm outward. Move the left palm in a circle upward
to in front of the right shoulder, palm inward. At the same time,
move the left foot back close to the right foot and keep them 10-20
centimetres apart, toes forward. Look at the right palm. (Fig. 120)

(4) Turn the upper part of the body to the left and shift the
weight to the left leg. Move both palms to the right, the left past
the face and the right past the abdomen in vertical circles. The
upper part of the body and the eyes follow the left hand. (Fig.
121)

(5) Continue to turn the upper part of the body to the left
and move the right foot one step to the right side, toes forward.
While the hands are waved like clouds to the left side of the body,

Fig. 118

Fig. 119

Fig. 120

Fig. 121

gradually turn over the palms, left palm outward and right palm inward. Look at the left palm. (Fig. 122)

(6) Turn the upper part of the body to the right and shift the weight to the right leg. Move the left foot close to the right foot, and keep them 10-20 centimetres apart. Move the hands in vertical circles simultaneously, right palm to the right past the face and left palm to the right past the abdomen. While they are moved to the right side of the body, the palms are gradually turned over. Both the upper body and the eyes follow the right palm. (Figs. 123-124)

(7) Repeat the movements in (4) to (6). (Figs. 125-128)

Points for attention: Move both feet parallel to the right. Make the steps lightly, inner side of the ball of the foot on the floor first. The whole exercise should be done evenly, steadily and continuously. Use the waist as the axis and keep the upper body upright. While moving the palms, the fingers of the upper palm should not be higher than the eyebrow, and those of the lower palm not lower than the crotch. Do not turn the palms over suddenly.

21. Part Horse's Mane on Both Sides

(1) Shift the weight to the left leg, and turn the upper part of the body to the left. Continue to wave the palms like clouds to the left and turn them over as if holding a ball in front of the body. Raise the right foot lightly at the same time. Look at the left palm. (Fig. 129)

(2) Turn the upper body slightly to the right and move the right foot one step forward to the right to form the right bow step (about 30 centimetres between the feet). Move the hands separately, the right upward to eye level and palm obliquely up, and the left downward by the left hip, palm down and fingers forward. Look at the right palm. (Fig. 130)

(3) Sit back and turn the upper body to the right with the toes of the right foot outward. Turn down the right arm and turn up the left arm as if holding a ball in front of the chest. At the same time, move the left foot to the inner side of the right foot. Look at the right palm. (Figs. 131-132)

(4) Turn the upper body to the left and move the left foot

Fig. 122

Fig. 123

Fig. 124

Fig. 125

Fig. 126

Fig. 127

Fig. 128

Fig. 129

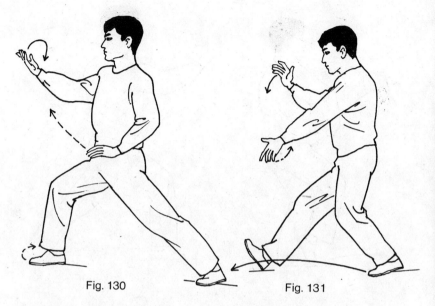

Fig. 130   Fig. 131

one step forward to the left to form the left bow step (about 30 centimetres between the feet). Move the hands separately, the left upward to eye level with palm obliquely up, and the right downward by the right hip with fingers forward. Look at the left palm. (Fig. 133)

Points for attention: When separating the hands in the holding a ball posture, the movements should be more extended, with the forearms slightly and obliquely outward and the waist turned with a greater amplitude than the warding off movement. So the feet should be spread farther apart. In executing the bow step, separation of the hands should be more coordinated with the bending of the legs. Extend the heel outward while straightening the rear leg with an angle of 45-60 degrees between the feet. Similar movements should also be executed in this way.

22. Pat High on Horse

(1) Move the right foot half a step forward, ball of foot on the floor. Extend the left palm slightly outward and move the right palm from below backward to shoulder level, palm up. Look

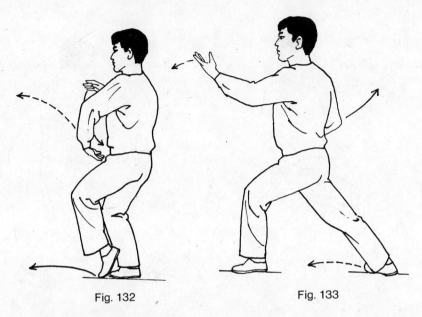

<table>
<tr><td>Fig. 132</td><td>Fig. 133</td></tr>
</table>

ahead. (Fig. 134)

(2) Shift the weight backward and land the right foot firmly on the floor. Turn the upper body slightly to the right and then to the left and skip the left foot slightly forward, ball of foot on the floor to form the left empty step. Drop the left hand down in front of the waist, palm up and fingers forward. Move the right palm past the ear and push it forward, palm obliquely forward and fingers to eye level. Look at the right palm. (Fig. 135)

Points for attention: When executing the follow-up step, sitting back and skipping the foot, turn the waist naturally and slightly to the left or right. Do not bend forward, protrude the buttocks or rise and fall suddenly.

23. Kick with Right Heel

(1) Turn the upper body to the right and lift the left foot lightly. Move the right palm backward to the right and turn the left palm over and downward to draw a circle forward and to the left. (Fig. 136)

(2) Move the left foot half a step forward to the left, heel on

Fig. 134

Fig. 135

the floor. At the same time, turn the left forearm outward, palm up and slightly backward. Thread the right palm forward over the left forearm. Look at the right palm. (Fig. 137)

(3) Land the left foot, shift the weight forward and bend the left leg forward. Move the right palm in a circle upward and forward and the left palm in a circle downward and backward, right palm down and left palm up. Look at the right palm. (Fig. 138)

(4) Move the right foot to the inner side of the left foot, toes on the floor (or not on the floor). Turn the waist slightly to the left and then to the right. Continue to move the hand in circles, the right palm downward and the left palm upward simultaneously and cross the wrists when they are in front of the chest (right palm outside), both palms inward. Look ahead to the right. (Fig. 139)

(5) Bend the left leg slightly and stand on it firmly. Raise the right foot, kick it slowly forward to the right (west and 30 degrees by north), toes flexed and force focused on the heel. Move the

Fig. 136

Fig. 137

Fig. 138

Fig. 139

palms separately in curves, one to the right forward and the other to the left backward, elbow slightly bent and wrist at shoulder level, palms outward. The right arm faces the right leg. Look at the right palm. (Fig. 140)

Points for attention: Coordinate the movement of the palms with the turn of the waist. The lines of movement of the palms (horizontal circle and vertical circle) should be connected and the movements should be circular and smooth. Move the palms and legs obliquely forward and backward in arcs. Do not push them straight or abruptly. Kick evenly and steadily. Keep the upper body upright. Do not bend the waist or lower the head. Do not hold your breath.

24. Strike Opponent's Ears with Both Fists

(1) Move the right shank back to bend the knee horizontally, toes down naturally. Turn the left forearm outward and move the left palm upward and forward in an arc and then drop it downward. Turn the right palm over and upward, both palms above the right knee. Look straight ahead. (Fig. 141)

(2) Land the right foot forward (west and 30 degrees by north), heel on the floor. Drop both palms and clench them into fists slowly at the hips. Look ahead. (Fig. 142)

(3) Land the right foot firmly on the floor, and shift the weight forward to form the right bow step. Sweep the fists from both sides upward and forward to ear level, knuckles of both hands down and a head width apart. Keep the arms like pincers. Look ahead. (Fig. 143)

Points for attention: Do not lower the head or bend the waist. Do not raise the ears or the elbows. Keep it in the same direction as the Kick with Right Heel Exercise, that is, due west by north.

25. Kick with Left Heel

(1) Shift the weight backward, toes of the right foot raised and slightly outward. Change the fists into palms and separate them to the two sides, palms outward. Look at the left palm. (Fig. 144)

(2) Shift the weight forward, place the left foot by the inner side of the right foot, toes on the floor (or not on the floor), and turn the waist slightly to the right and then to the left. At the

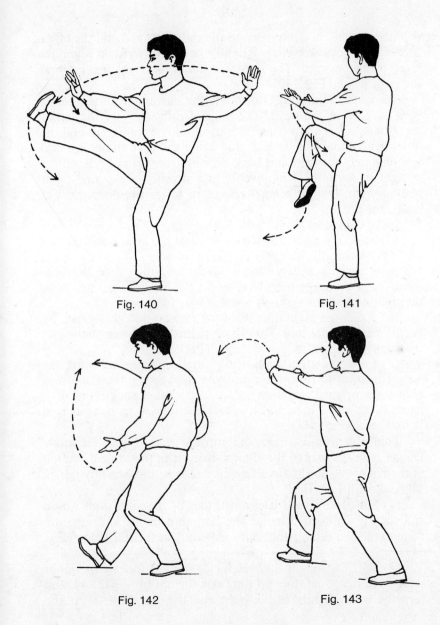

Fig. 140

Fig. 141

Fig. 142

Fig. 143

same time, move the hands simultaneously in arcs from both sides downward and inward and cross them in front of the chest (left palm outside), palms inward. Look ahead to the left. (Fig. 145)

(3) Bend the right leg slightly and stand on it firmly. Raise the left knee and kick with foot forward to the left slowly (west and 30 degrees by south) toes flexed and force focused on the heel. Move both hands simultaneously, one to the left forward and the other to the right backward in arcs, elbows bent slightly and wrists at shoulder level. The left arm faces the left leg. Look at the left palm. (Fig. 146)

Points for attention: The same as for the Kick with Right Heel Exercise. The only difference is the direction.

26. Strike with Hidden Fist

(1) Move the left foot back to the inner side of the right foot, toes on the floor, and turn the upper body slightly to the right. Move the palms from both sides upward and inward and raise them in front of the head. At the same time, change the right palm into a fist, both palms inward. Look ahead. (Fig. 147)

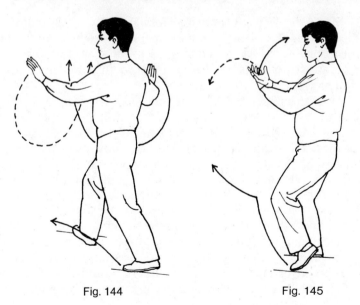

Fig. 144   Fig. 145

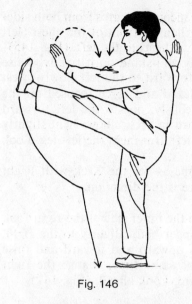

Fig. 146   Fig. 147

(2) Move the left foot one step forward to the left (south-west), heel on the floor, and turn the upper body to the right, both arms turned outward. At the same time, lower them to the right side of the waist, right fist in the left palm, both palms up. Look down and to the right. (Fig. 148)

(3) Turn the upper body to the left, shift the weight to the left, bend the left leg forward and straighten the right leg to form the left bow step. Withdraw the left palm to the left side of the waist as the waist turns to the left, knuckles down. As the body turns, the right fist strikes forward in a straight and quick blow at abdomen level, knuckles up. Look at the right fist. (Fig. 149)

Points for attention: The stance is the left bow step (west by north) and the blow is struck due west. Relax the shoulders, drop the elbows, and extend the shoulders after striking. If the force is quickly released, attention should be paid to the movement of the whole body and the release of force from the waist and legs. The bow step should be larger and the shoulders should be extended farther forward. The forearm should be jerked quickly and loose-

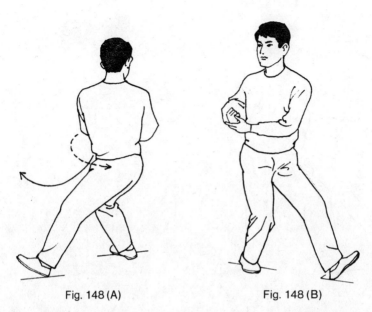

Fig. 148 (A)   Fig. 148 (B)

ly. The fist should not go above shoulder level. All movements should be well coordinated, harmonious, natural and continuous.

27. Needle at Sea Bottom

(1) Move the right foot half a step forward to behind the left foot, ball of foot on the floor first, and then the whole foot. Turn the upper body to the right, and shift the weight backward to the right leg, left foot raised lightly. Change the left fist into a palm and move it in a horizontal arc to the left and forward, palm down, and open the right fist, move it down and past the right side of the body upward to the right ear, palm inward. Look ahead. (Figs. 150-151)

(2) Turn the upper body to the left. Cut down with the right palm, fingers obliquely forward and downward and palm to the left. Move the left hand in a curve to the left and press it by the left hip, fingers forward. Move the left foot half a step forward, ball of foot on the floor to form the left empty step. Lower the waist and drop the shoulders. Look down and forward. (Fig. 152)

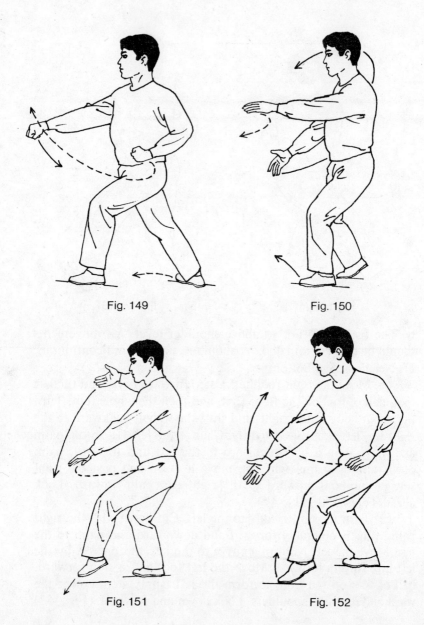

Fig. 149

Fig. 150

Fig. 151

Fig. 152

Points for attention: The steps should be coordinated with the turn of the waist. In the final position, extend the right shoulder forward and bend the upper the body slightly forward.

28. Flash Arm

(1) Turn the upper body slightly to the right, left leg raised. Move the palms upward, left palm close to the inner side of the right wrist. Look ahead. (Fig. 153)

(2) Land the left foot forward and shift the weight forward to form the left bow step. Turn the right palm forward to stop at the right side of the forehead, palm obliquely up and fingers to the left. Push the left palm forward past the chest, palm forward at nose level. Look at the left palm. (Fig. 154)

Points for attention: In raising the hands, do not shrug shoulders or raise elbows. In the final position, relax the waist forward and downward. Do not protrude the right hip.

Part V

29. Kick with Right and Left Foot

(1) Shift the weight backward, toes of the left foot fully inward, and turn the upper body to the right backward. Move the palms in arcs to both sides, palms outward. Look ahead to the right. (Fig. 155)

(2) Shift the weight to the left and withdraw the right foot, toes on the floor (or not on the floor). Move both hands in arcs downward in front of the body and cross them at wrists in front of the abdomen and move them up with an oblique cross in front of the chest (right palm outside), both palms inward. Look ahead to the right (due east by south). (Figs. 156 (A) and 156 (B))

(3) Bend the left leg slightly, stand on it firmly, and raise the right leg to kick slowly forward to the right (due east by south), instep flat. Move the hands simultaneously, one to the right forward and the other to the left backward, both palms outward and wrists at shoulder level, elbows slightly bent. The right arm faces the right leg. Look at the right palm. (Fig. 157)

(4) Bend the right knee and land the right foot forward and to the right (southeast), heel on the floor. Turn up the right arm, and draw the right palm slightly backward. Lower the left palm,

Fig. 153

Fig. 154

Fig. 155

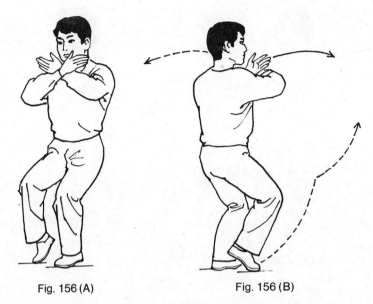

<table>
<tr><td>Fig. 156 (A)</td><td>Fig. 156 (B)</td></tr>
</table>

Fig. 156 (A)   Fig. 156 (B)

move it in an arc past the left side of the waist forward and upward and thread it forward over the right forearm, palm forward. Look at the left palm. (Fig. 158)

(5) Land the right foot on the floor, shift the weight forward, and straighten the left leg. Move the left palm upward and forward in an arc, palm down. Move the right palm in an arc downward and backward, palm up. Look at the left palm. (Fig. 159)

(6) Withdraw the left foot to the inner side of the right foot, toes on the floor (or not on the floor), and turn the waist slightly to the right and then to the left. Continue to move the hands in arcs, the left palm downward and the right palm upward. Cross the palms at wrists in front of the chest (the left outside), both palms inward. Look ahead and to the right (due east by north). (Fig. 160)

(7) Bend the right leg slightly and stand on it firmly. Raise the left knee and kick with the left foot forward to the left (due east by north) slowly, instep flat. Move the hands simultaneously,

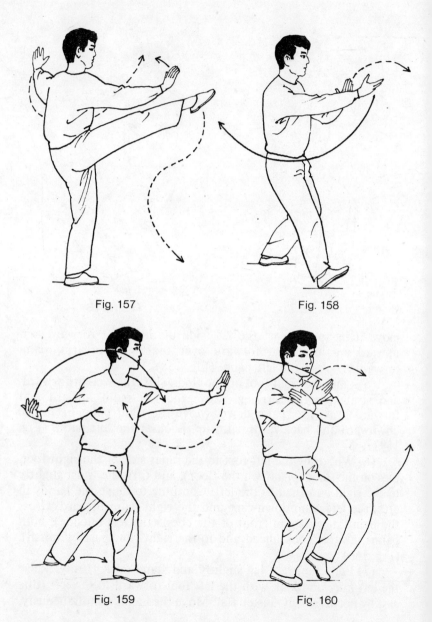

Fig. 157

Fig. 158

Fig. 159

Fig. 160

one to the left forward and the other to the right backward in arcs, palms both outward and wrists at shoulder level, elbows slightly bent. The left arm faces the left leg. Look at the left palm. (Fig. 161)

Points for attention: Refer to the Kick with Right Heel Exercise

30. Brush Knee with Left and Right Bow Step (Two)

(1) Bend the left shank, land the left foot by the inner side of the right foot, and turn the upper body to the right. Turn the right palm and lift it up to head level. Move the left palm in an arc, as the body turns, upward and to the right and stop it in front of the right shoulder, palm down. Look at the right palm. (Fig. 162)

(2) Turn the upper body to the left, move the left foot one step forward to the left and shift the weight forward to form the left bow step (about 30 centimetres between the feet). Circle the left palm downward around the left knee and press it by the left hip, fingers forward. Bend the right arm and push it forward past the ear, palm forward at nose level. Look at the right palm fingers. (Fig. 163)

(3) Shift the weight backward, toes of the left foot raised and outward, and turn the upper part of the body to the left. Turn both forearms outward, right palm to the left and left palm up. (Fig. 164)

(4) Move the right foot forward to the right, and repeat the previous movements from (1) to (3) on the right side. (Figs. 165-166)

Points for attention: While pushing the palms, extend the shoulders slightly forward, relax the waist, drop the shoulders and keep the upper body upright.

31. Step Forward to Strike

(1) Shift the weight backward, toes of the right foot raised and outward. Turn the left palm up and move it back slightly. Bend the right elbow and thread the palm forward over the left forearm, palm obliquely outward. Look ahead. (Fig. 167)

(2) Land the right foot, shift the weight forward, and turn the body to the right. Move the right palm forward from the left,

Fig. 161

Fig. 162

Fig. 163

Fig. 164

Fig. 165

Fig. 166

Fig. 167

Fig. 168

then to the right in an arc, and the left palm to the right and backward in an arc and pull it back in front of the abdomen. Look at the right palm. (Fig. 168)

(3) Move the left foot one step forward. Move the right palm in an arc outward and clench the fist by the right side of the waist, knuckles down. Move the left palm to the left and then forward in an arc, and clench it as it stops in front at shoulder level, knuckles up and thumb side obliquely inward. Look at the left fist. (Fig. 169)

(4) Land the left foot and shift the weight forward to form the left bow step. The right fist strikes forward from the waist at shoulder level, with knuckles thumb side up. Place the left fist slightly backward under the right wrist, thumb side down. Look at the right fist. (Fig. 170)

Points for attention: The palm movements should be continuous and smooth. Turn the waist first to the right and then to the left when striking forward with the right fist.

32. Apparent Close-Up

(1) Move the right foot half a step forward, ball of foot on the floor. At the same time, open both fists so that the palms face obliquely upward. Look straight ahead. (Fig. 171)

(2) Shift the weight backward, place the right foot fully on the floor, and bend the left leg forward to form the left bow step. Move the palms slowly apart until they come to the front of the chest at shoulder width. While forearms are being turned inward, move the hands downward to in front of the abdomen and then press them forward, palms forward and wrists at shoulder level. Look ahead. (Figs. 172-174)

Points for attention: When moving the palms apart, withdraw and turn down the palms at the same time. Use the elbows to draw the forearms backward. There should be a clear distinction between the empty and the solid when shifting the weight. The pressing of the hands and the bending of the leg should be well coordinated and synchronized for the finish.

33. Wave Hands like Clouds, Left (Three)

(1) Shift the weight backward, toes of the left foot inward, and turn the upper body to the right. Move the right hand from

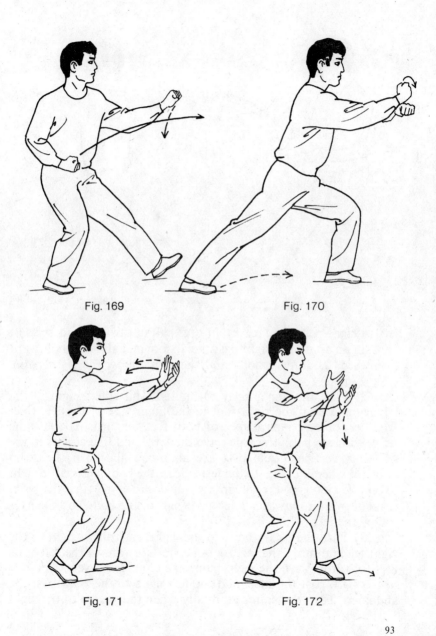

Fig. 169

Fig. 170

Fig. 171

Fig. 172

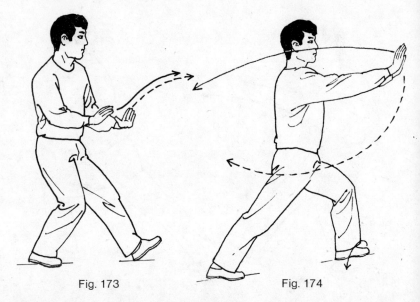

Fig. 173   Fig. 174

left to right past the face in an arc, palm outward, and the left hand in an arc to the right past the abdomen, palm from outward to inward. The upper body and the eyes follow the right palm. (Fig. 175)

(2) Turn the upper body to the left, shift the weight to the left leg and land the right foot to the inner side of the left foot, 10-20 centimetres apart, toes of both feet forward. At the same time, with the palm inward, wave the left hand like clouds to the left in a vertical circle past the abdomen and turn the palm outward when it comes to the left side of the body. Wave the right palm like clouds to the left in a vertical circle and turn the palm from outward to inward. The upper part of the body and the eyes follow the left palm. (Figs. 176-178)

(3) Turn the upper body to the right, shift the weight to the right leg and move the left foot one step forward to the left side, toes forward. Wave the right palm like clouds in a vertical circle to the right past the face, and the left palm to the right past the abdomen. Turn the palms gradually when they come to the right

Fig. 175

Fig. 176

Fig. 177

Fig. 178

95

side of the body. The upper body and eyes follow the right palm. (Figs. 178-179)

(4) Turn the upper body to the left, shift the weight to the left leg, and place the right foot to the inner side of the left foot (10-20 centimetres apart), toes of both feet forward. At the same time, wave the left palm like clouds past the face to the left in a vertical circle, and the right palm past the abdomen to the left in a vertical circle. When they come to the left side of the body, turn the left palm outward and the right palm inward. The upper part of the body and the eyes follow the left palm. (Figs. 180-181)

(5) Repeat the previous movements, but turn the toes of the right foot about 45 degrees inward in the final position. (Figs. 182-185)

Points for attention: The same as those for Wave Hands Like Clouds, Right, but in the left direction. When withdrawing the right-shaped step for the third time, turn the toes of the right foot inward to facilitate the connection with the following movement.

34. Turn Right to Strike

(1) Shift the weight to the right, move the left foot one step backward (northwest), and bend the right leg to form the right bow step. Turn the left palm upward and move it in an arc to the front of the body and then back to the front of the abdomen. Turn the right palm downward and move it forward over the left forearm at shoulder level. Look at the right palm. (Fig. 186)

(2) Shift the weight backward to the left leg, move the right foot to the inner side of the left foot, toes on the floor, and turn the upper body to the left. Drop the right palm and clench it in front of the abdomen, knuckles forward and thumb side to the left. Move the left palm in an arc to the left and upward to the front of the body, and turn it down to the inner side of the right forearm. The head follows the body's turn. Look ahead. (Fig. 187)

(3) Turn the body slightly to the right, move the right foot to the original place (southeast), shift the weight forward, bend the right leg and straighten the left leg to form the right bow step. Raise the right fist past the left part of the chest to strike forward and upward, knuckles obliquely outward at nose level. Place the left palm on the inner side of the right forearm. Look at the right

Fig. 179

Fig. 180

Fig. 181

Fig. 182

Fig. 183

Fig. 184

Fig. 185

Fig. 186

Fig. 187   Fig. 188

fist. (Fig. 188)

Points for attention: Do not twist or cross the legs when executing the bow step. Other points are the same as those for Turn Left to Strike.

35. Work at Shuttles on Both Sides

(1) Shift the weight backward, toes of the right foot raised and turned inward, and turn the upper body slightly to the left. Thread the left palm forward over the right forearm, palm obliquely down. Open the right fist and move it slightly backward, palm obliquely up. (Fig. 189)

(2) Turn the upper body slightly further to the left, land the foot, and shift the weight to the right leg. Rub with the left palm forward to the left, and place the right palm under the inner side of the left elbow. The palms face each other obliquely. Look at the left palm. (Fig. 190)

(3) Turn the upper body to the right. Pull the palms back downward, the right palm to the right hip, palm up, and the left palm to the front of the abdomen, palm obliquely down. At the

Fig. 189   Fig. 190

same time, move the left foot to the inner side of the right foot. Look ahead and to the right. (Fig. 191)

(4) Move the left foot one step forward to the left (northeast), and shift the weight forward to form the left bow step. Turn the left forearm outward and the right forearm inward, and lift both palms to the front of the chest, fingers of the right hand lightly touching the inner side of the left wrist, and move them in a horizontal circle from right forward, left palm obliquely up and right palm obliquely down to shoulder level. Look at the left palm. (Fig. 192)

(5) Turn the upper body to the left. Bend the left arm at the elbow and move the left palm in a horizontal circle to the left and backward, palm obliquely up. Place the right palm on the inner side of the left wrist. At the same time, move the right foot half a step forward, ball of foot on the floor. Look at the left palm. (Fig. 193)

(6) Land the right foot, shift the weight backward to the right leg, raise the left foot and turn the upper body to the right.

Fig. 191   Fig. 192

Withdraw the right palm from the inner side of the left forearm to the front of the chest. Turn the left forearm inward, and turn the left palm obliquely forward. Look ahead and to the right. (Fig. 194)

(7) Move the left foot one step forward (northeast), and bend the left leg to form the left bow step (about 30 centimetres between the feet). Turn the upper body to the left. Place the left palm forward and above the left side of the forehead, palm obliquely up. Push the right palm forward, palm forward at nose level. Look at the right palm. (Fig. 195)

(8) Shift the weight backward, toes of the left foot raised and turned inward, and turn the upper body to the right. Turn the left arm outward and drop it to the front of the body, palm obliquely up. Move the right palm slightly back and then thread it forward over the left forearm. (Fig. 196)

(9) Land the left foot, shift the weight forward to the left leg, and turn the upper body slightly to the right. Rub forward to the right with the right palm and place the left palm under the inner

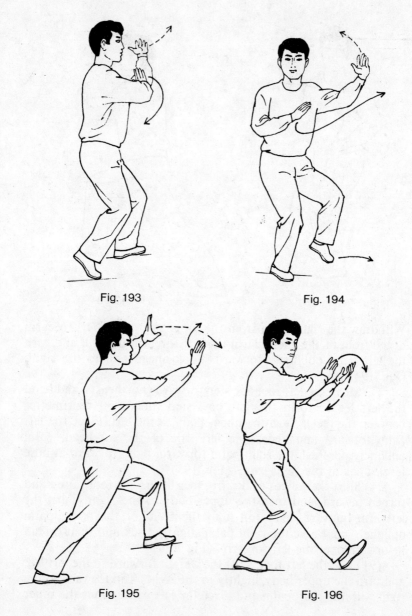

Fig. 193

Fig. 194

Fig. 195

Fig. 196

side of the right elbow, palms facing each other obliquely. Look at the right palm. (Fig. 197)

(10) Turn the upper body to the left. Pull the palms back and downward, left palm to the left hip with palm up, and the right palm to the front of the abdomen, palm obliquely down. At the same time, withdraw the right foot to the inner side of the left foot. Look ahead and to the left. (Fig. 198)

(11) Move the right foot one step forward to the right (southeast), and shift the weight forward to form the right bow step. Turn the forearms, both palms up, and move them back to the front of the chest, fingers of the left palm touching the inner side of the right wrist, and draw a horizontal circle from left forward as the weight is shifted forward, right palm obliquely up and left palm obliquely down at shoulder level. Look at the right palm. (Fig. 199)

(12) Turn the upper body to the right and move the left foot half a step forward, ball of foot on the floor. Bend the right arm and move it in a horizontal circle to the right and backward. Keep the left palm on the inner side of the right wrist. Look at the right palm. (Fig. 200)

(13) Land the left foot, shift the weight to the left leg, raise the right foot slightly and turn the upper body to the left. Place the left palm in front of the chest and turn the right forearm inward, palm obliquely forward. Look ahead and to the right. (Fig. 201)

(14) Move the right foot one step forward, bend the right leg to form the right bow step (about 30 centimetres between the feet), and turn the upper body to the right. Place the right palm in front above the right side of the forehead, palm obliquely up. Push the left palm forward to nose level, palm forward. Look at the left palm. (Fig. 202)

Points for attention: The movements of the hands and feet should be well coordinated. The turning of the feet inward (parallel to the central line) should be in harmony with the threading of the palms; the bending of the legs with the rubbing of the palms; the pulling of the palms with the withdrawing of the feet; the turning over of the palms with the stepping forward

Fig. 197

Fig. 198

Fig. 199

Fig. 200

Fig. 201   Fig. 202

and bending of the legs; the moving of the palms in horizontal circles with the follow-up steps; the turning over of the palms with sitting back; and the pushing of the palms with the bending of the legs and stepping forward. The steps are about 30 centimetres long. Keep the upper body and hips upright and avoid raising the elbows, leaning the body, or twisting the hips.

36. Step Back and Thread Palm

(1) Shift the weight backward to the left leg, toes of the right foot raised, and turn the upper body to the left. Move the left palm to the left and backward in an arc until it comes to the left side of the waist, palm down. Turn the right forearm outward and drop the right palm to the front of the body, palm obliquely up to the left. Look at the right palm. (Fig. 203)

(2) Raise the right foot and move it backward (due west) past the inner side of the left foot and bend the left leg to form the left bow step. Press the right palm downward to under the left elbow. Turn the left palm upward, move it to the waist and thread it forward over the right forearm to eye level. Look at the left

105

Fig. 203　　　　　　　　Fig. 204

palm. (Fig. 204)

Points for attention: Sit back fully when shifting the weight to the rear leg, withdraw the foot gently and retreat steadily. The movements of the upper and lower limbs should be coordinated, but the hand movements should not be too quick.

Part VI

37. Press Down Palms with Empty Step

(1) Shift the weight backward, toes of the left foot turned inward, and turn the upper part of the body to the right backward. At the same time, withdraw the right palm to the front of the abdomen and place the left palm in front of the left side of the forehead. Look straight ahead. (Fig. 205)

(2) Shift the weight backward to the left leg, and raise the right foot, toes turned forward to form the right empty step. Lower the upper body and bend it slightly forward. Press the left palm downward above the right knee, palm down and thumb inward. Press the right palm by the side of the right hip, fingers

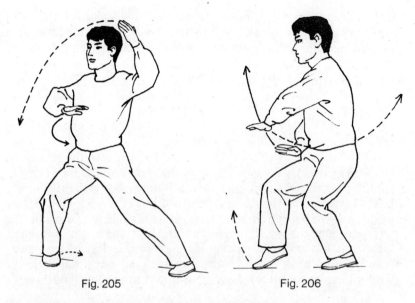

Fig. 205   Fig. 206

forward. Look down and forward. (Fig. 206)

Points for attention: When executing the empty step, move the right foot slightly to the right, and relax the waist and hips. When pressing the palms, extend the shoulders and turn the waist. Do not lower the head or bend forward.

38. Stand on One Leg and Hold out Palm

Stand on the left leg, slightly bent, bend the right leg and raise it, toes naturally down. At the same time, turn the upper body to the left, turn the right palm up and hold it in front, palm up and wrist at chest level. Move the left palm to the left and upward in an arc and hold it by the left side at chest level, palm outward and fingers obliquely upward. Look at the front palm. (Fig. 207)

Points for attention: Standing, turning the waist, and holding the palm should all be well coordinated. In the final position, relax the waist, draw in the chest, drop the shoulders, elbows and wrists, and breathe gently.

39. Push Forearm with Horse-Riding Step

(1) Land the right foot in front, shift the weight to the right leg, and turn the upper body to the right. Turn the right arm inward and the palm in an arc downward to the right. Turn the left arm outward and the left palm upward and to the right in an arc. Look straight ahead. (Fig. 208)

(2) Withdraw the left foot to the inner side of the right foot. Turn the right palm upward and hold it by the side of the right ear. Change the left palm into a fist and place it in front of the chest, knuckles up. Look forward. (Fig. 209)

(3) Move the left foot forward to the left (southwest), shift the weight slightly forward to form the semi-horse stance (weight slightly to the right leg), and turn the upper body slightly to the left. Move the left forearm downward past the abdomen before pushing it forward, and bend the left arm slightly to stop by the left side of the body, knuckles up and fist above the left knee. Drop the left palm by the inner side of the left elbow, palm forward, and push the left arm forward (the push may be done with an explosive force). Look ahead and to the left (southwest).

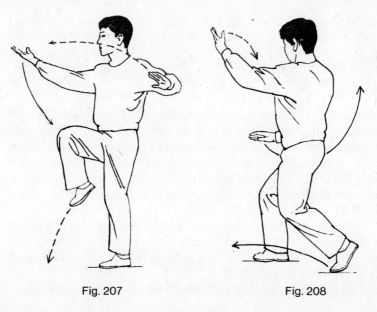

Fig. 207   Fig. 208

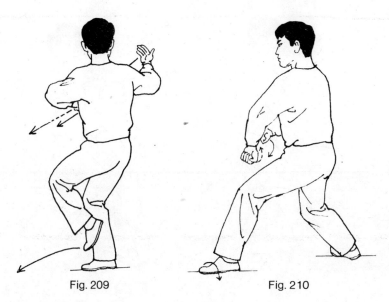

Fig. 209 Fig. 210

(Fig. 210)

Points for attention: The forward steps should be executed with the heel on the floor first, and then the whole foot on the floor as the weight shifts forward. In the final position, face the southwest, move the waist forward and downward to keep the steps stable, and the upper body upright. If the explosive force is released, it should originate from the waist and legs. The angle between the feet in the semi-horse stance should not be greater than 90 degrees. The weight is slightly on the rear leg. The crotch should be circular and the rear knee slightly inward.

40. Turn Body with Big Strokes

(1) Shift the weight backward and turn the upper body slightly to the right, toes of the left foot outward. Open the left fist and turn both palms to the right simultaneously and move them slightly backward. Look forward. (Fig. 211)

(2) Turn the upper body to the left, land the left foot, shift the weight forward, and move the right foot forward to the inner side of the left foot (feet parallel and about 10 centimetres apart).

Fig. 211   Fig. 212

Raise the body slightly upward and keep the weight on the left leg. Raise both palms to shoulder level, the right palm up, and the left palm bent in front and outward. Look at the right palm. (Figs. 212-213)

(3) Pivot on the ball of foot of the right foot, heel outward, bend the knee to squat and shift the weight to the right leg. Turn the upper body to the left and move the left foot backward (northwest). As the body turns, pull both palms horizontally to the front of the body in a gentle stroke, the right palm extended southeast to shoulder level and the left palm stopping at the inner side of the right elbow, palms facing each other obliquely. Look at the right palm. (Figs. 214-215)

(4) Continue to turn the upper body to the left, shift the weight to the left leg, heel of the right foot turned outward to form a side bow step. As the body turns, pull both palms to the left horizontally in a gentle stroke, and at the same time gradually clench fists. Then relax the waist and drop the shoulders. Turn the left forearm outward and withdraw the left fist to the waist,

Fig. 213

Fig. 214

Fig. 215

knuckles down, while turning the right forearm outward and dropping the elbow, right fist at chest level in front. Bend the right arm into a curve, knuckles obliquely forward. Look at the right fist. (Figs. 216 (A) and 216 (B))

Points for attention: The steps, body turns and hand movements should be well connected and coordinated, with the waist as the axis. Face due south after the feet are placed together, and face southeast after moving the step backward, with the rear foot obliquely facing northeast. In the final position, face northeast to form the side bow step (feet parallel forward, the same width as the bow step, left leg bent and right leg straightened), bend and drop the elbows. The head follows the body's turn.

41. Sweep Palm with Crouch Stance

(1) Turn the upper body to the right and shift the weight to the right leg. Bend the right arm and move upward in an arc, with the right fist stopping in front of the right side of the forehead, knuckles inward. Thread the left fist backward behind the body, knuckles forward. Look forward. (Fig. 217)

Fig. 216 (A)   Fig. 216 (B)

(2) Turn the toes of the left foot outward and toes of the right foot inward, shift the weight to the left and turn the upper body to the left. Open the left fist while it is turned up and moved to the front of the body in an arc, palm obliquely down. Open the right fist and move it backward and downward in an arc, palm gradually going from backward to forward. The head follows the body's turn. Look forward. (Fig. 218)

(3) Move the right foot a half step forward to the right side behind the left foot, ball of foot on the floor to form the T-shaped step. Swing the right palm forward and downward past the outer side of the right hip, palm obliquely forward at abdomen level. Put the fingers of the left palm at the inner side of the right forearm, palm obliquely down and thumb inward. Face the northwest. Look down and ahead. (Fig. 219 (A) and 219 (B))

(4) Land the right foot, turn the upper body to the right, shift the weight to the right leg and raise the left foot gently. Move the right palm upward and to the right in an arc and change it into the hook hand in front to the right, left palm remaining at the

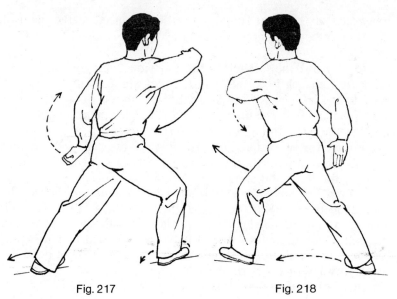

Fig. 217   Fig. 218

Fig. 219 (A)

Fig. 219 (B)

inner side of the right forearm until it is placed at the bend of the right elbow, palm inward. Look at the right hook. (Figs. 220-221)

(5) Extend the left leg to the left side (west by south) and bend the right leg to form the left crouch stance. Turn the upper body to the left. Lower the left palm and thread it forward past the abdomen along the inner side of the left leg, palm to the right. Look at the left palm. (Figs. 222-223)

Points for attention: The turning of the feet inward and outward should be in harmony with the body's turn. The movement of the left hand should not be too great when it draws the arc behind the body. In executing the follow-up step, close the hips, bend the leg, and raise the right foot gently. In the crouch stance, extend the left leg first and then turn the body to thread the palm. The right foot should be fully extended (a half squat for the elderly). Both feet should be on the floor. Do not bend the trunk forward or lower the head.

42. Step Forward to Cross Fists

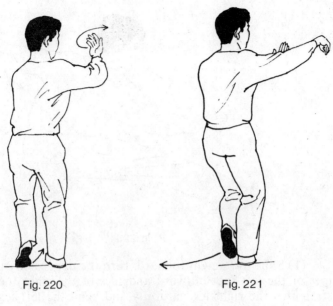

Fig. 220   Fig. 221

Fig. 222

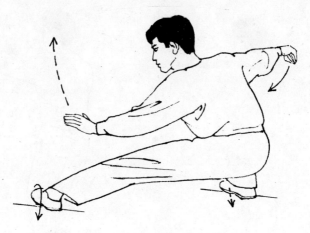

Fig. 223

(1) Shift the weight forward, turn the upper body to the left, toes of the left foot outward and toes of the right foot inward, straighten the right leg naturally and bend the left leg forward. Move the left palm upward and forward to shoulder level. Turn the right arm and drop it, fingers of the hook up behind the body. Look at the left palm. (Fig. 224)

(2) Move the right foot one step forward, ball of foot on the floor to form the right empty step. Change the left palm into a fist and withdraw it slightly inward, knuckles outward. Change the right hook into a fist and move it forward and upward, knuckles inward. Cross the hands at wrists (right fist outside) at shoulder level, arms forming a circle. Look at the left fist. (Fig. 225)

Points for attention: Before rising from the crouch step, turn the toes of the left foot outward as much as possible and those of the right foot inward as much as possible while the body turns. Close the hips and step forward gently and steadily. In the final position, both the shoulders and hips should be relaxed.

43. Stand on One Leg to Mount Tiger

(1) Move the right foot one step backward to the right, shift the weight backward and turn the upper body to the right. Open

Fig. 224

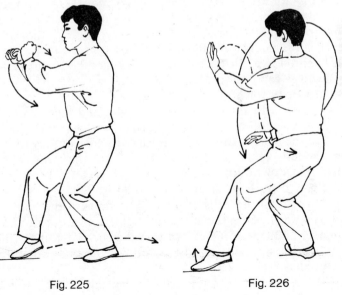

Fig. 225   Fig. 226

the right fist and move it downward and to the right in an arc until it stops outside the right hip, palm down. Open the left fist at the same time and move it slightly to the right in an arc as the body turns to the right. (Fig. 226)

(2) Raise the left foot and move it slightly to the right to form the left empty step, and turn the upper body to the left. Move the left palm past the abdomen in a curve to the left and press it by the left hip. Move the right palm upward in a curve past the front of the head and then downward to above the left side of the left leg, palm up. The head follows the body's turn. Look straight ahead. (Fig. 227)

(3) Stand on the right leg, slightly bent, and raise the left leg with the knee slightly bent and instep flat in front of the body. Move the right palm forward and upward, palm obliquely to the left and wrist at shoulder level. Change the left palm into a hook hand and raise it backward to the left to shoulder level. Turn the upper body to the left. Look ahead and to the left (southwest). (Fig. 228)

Points for attention: In the final position, stand on the right leg, slightly bent; the left leg looks straight, but is not straight. It is naturally raised in front of the body, toes of the left foot slightly inward. The height differs from person to person. The right hand faces the left foot. The upper body turns to the southwest. Keep it natural and relaxed.

44. Turn Body for Lotus Leg Swing

(1) Turn the upper body to the right, and land the left foot outside the right foot, toes pointing rightward. Open the left hook and turn the palm up and swing it forward horizontally in a curve from the left behind to shoulder level. Turn the right palm over and pull it downward, to the right and backward horizontally with elbow bent. Look straight ahead. (Fig. 229)

(2) Pivot on the balls of both feet, and turn the body to the right backward. Move the left palm slightly inward, turn the right palm over and thread it forward past the chest and under the left elbow, both palms up. The head follows the body's turn. Look straight ahead. (Fig. 230)

(3) Continue to turn the body to the right to face due south.

Fig. 227

Fig. 228

Fig. 229

Move the right palm upward and to the right in an arc after threading from under the left elbow. At the same time, turn the right forearm inward, palm turned to the right and lifted up by the right side of the body at shoulder level. Move the left palm back from the inner side of the right arm to the front of the right shoulder, palm also turned to the right. Look at the right palm. (Fig. 231)

(4) Raise the right foot to swing outward to the left, upward and to the right in the shape of a Chinese fan, instep flat. At the same time, swing the palms from right to left and pat the right instep first with the left palm and then with the right palm. Look at both palms. (Fig. 232)

Points for attention: Land the left foot not too far from the right foot, bend both legs slightly, balls of feet grinding the floor, and turn the body 270 degrees. Do not shake the body. The threading of the palms should be in harmony with the body's turn. In swinging the foot, raise the right leg and bend the trunk slightly forward. Don't be nervous. The elderly may not pat the

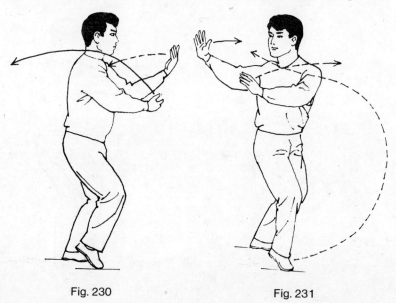

Fig. 230   Fig. 231

instep.

45. Draw Bow to Shoot Tiger

(1) Bend the right shank and move it backward, and raise the right foot on the right side of the body, toes naturally down. Stand on the left leg, slightly bent, and turn the upper body to the left. Swing both palms to the left, the left to the left side of the body and the right to the front of the left shoulder, both palms to the left and at shoulder level. Look at the left palm. (Fig. 233)

(2) Turn the upper body slightly to the right, and land the right foot on the right side (due west slightly by north), both palms down. Look forward. (Fig. 234)

(3) Turn the upper body to the right and shift the weight to the right to form the right bow step. Move both palms in arcs simultaneously downward and to the right and change them into fists when the palms come to the right side of the body. Then turn the upper body to the left and move the left fist past the face to strike forward to the left (southwest) to nose level, knuckles obliquely backward and thumb obliquely down. Move the right

Fig. 232

Fig. 233

back to before the right side of the forehead, elbow bent, palm outward and thumb obliquely down. Look at the left fist. (Figs. 235-236)

Points for attention: When swinging the hands to the right, turn the head and waist simultaneously, and look at the right fist. In the final position, relax and lower the waist and turn it back slightly, but do not turn the right knee inward or twist the hips to the left. Turn the head southwest in the same direction as the left fist. The bow step is executed slightly by northwest.

46. Turn to Strike, Parry and Punch, Right

(1) Bend the left leg and shift the weight backward, toes of the right foot inward while turning the upper body to the left. Open the left fist, turn the palm upward and lower it past the front of the body to the left side of the waist. Open the right fist and thread the palm forward over the left forearm, and rub forward with the palm forward and downward. Look first at the right palm and then straight ahead. (Figs. 237-238)

(2) Move the right foot back to the inner side of the left foot.

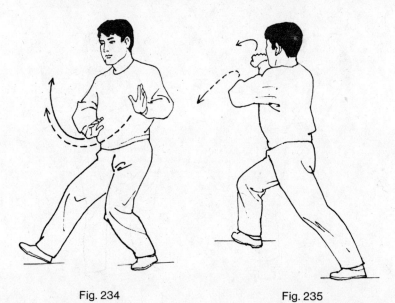

Fig. 234   Fig. 235

Fig. 236

Fig. 237

Move the left palm in an arc on the left side back to the front of the chest, palm down. Change the right palm into a fist and withdraw it downward to the front of the left ribs, knuckles up. Look forward. (Fig. 239)

(3) Skip the right foot forward, heel on the floor and toes outward, and turn the upper body to the right. Turn the right fist over forward (due west) to chest level, knuckles down. Press the left palm by the left hip, fingers forward. Look at the right fist. (Fig. 240)

(4) Turn the upper body to the right, shift the weight forward, and move the left foot forward. Move the right fist in an arc to the right and place it by the right side of the waist, knuckles down. Move the left palm in an arc to the left and forward to execute a parry, palm obliquely down. Look at the left palm. (Fig. 241)

(5) Shift the weight forward, bend the left leg forward to form the left bow step, and turn the upper body to the left. Punch forward with the right fist, thumb up at chest level. Withdraw the

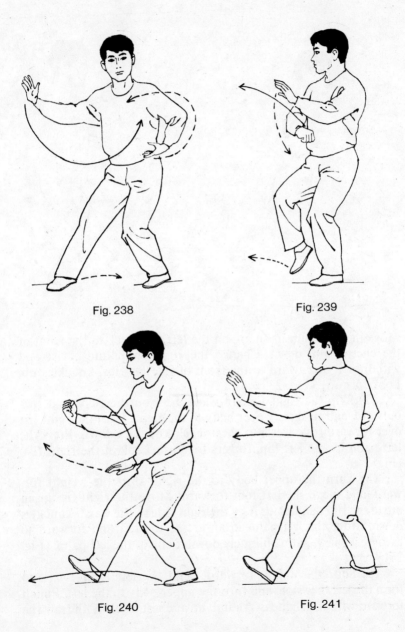

Fig. 238

Fig. 239

Fig. 240

Fig. 241

left palm to the inner side of the right forearm. Look at the right fist. (Fig. 242)

Points for attention: When withdrawing the right foot, first turn the toes back before moving the foot. When necessary, turn the toes of the left foot properly outward to facilitate the left body turn. Other points are the same as for Turn to Strike, Parry and Punch, Left, but in the opposite direction.

47. Ward off, Stroke, Push and Press, Right

(1) Shift the weight backward, toes of the left foot outward, and turn the upper body to the left. Move the left palm downward in an arc, palm up, and at the same time change the right fist into a palm and stretch it forward, palm down. Look ahead and to the left. (Fig. 243)

(2) Shift the weight forward, bend the left leg at the knee, and withdraw the right foot to the inner side of the left foot. At the same time, move the right palm downward in an arc, and the left palm backward and then turn it upward in an arc, both palms in front of the chest as if holding a ball (right palm below, palms

Fig. 242   Fig. 243

facing each other). Look at the left palm. (Fig. 244)

(3) Turn the upper body slightly to the right and move the right foot one step forward, and shift the weight forward to form the right bow step. Move the palms respectively upward and downward, the right forearm warding off in front at shoulder level and palm inward, and the left palm pressing by the left hip. Look at the right forearm. (Fig. 245)

(4) Turn the upper body slightly to the right while the right hand stretches forward, forearm turned inward, palm down, and left forearm turned outward, palm up, and move it upward past the abdomen and forward in an arc and to under the right forearm. Look at the right palm. (Fig. 246)

(5) Turn the upper body to the left, move the hands downward as if stroking a long beard, and past the abdomen to upper left backward in an arc, and lift it up until the left palm is obliquely up, wrist at shoulder level, right palm obliquely backward, and bend it horizontally in front of the chest. At the same time, shift the weight backward to the left leg. Look at the left

Fig. 244   Fig. 245

Fig. 246

palm. (Fig. 247)

(6) Turn the upper body to the right, and shift the weight forward to form the right bow step. Turn the left arm inward, elbow bent. Move the fingers of the left palm forward close to the inner side of the right wrist, palm forward, and push both hands slowly forward, right palm inward and arms forming a semicircle. Look at the right wrist. (Fig. 248)

(7) Extend the left palm over the right wrist and immediately move the palms apart to the two sides at shoulder width, palms down. Sit back, and shift the weight to the left leg, toes of the right foot raised. Bend both arms at the elbow and withdraw the palms to the front of the chest, palms forward and down. Look straight ahead. (Fig. 249)

(8) Land the right foot and bend the right leg forward to form the right bow step. Press the palms past the abdomen forward and upward, wrists at shoulder level and palms forward. Look straight ahead. (Fig. 250)

Points for attention: The same as those for Ward off, Stroke,

Fig. 247

Fig. 249

Fig. 248

Fig. 250

Push and Press, Left, but in the opposite direction.

48. Cross Hands

(1) Turn the upper body to the left, and shift the weight to the left, toes of the right foot inward. Swing the left palm horizontally forward past the face, and move the right palm to the right side at the same time, both palms forward. Look at the left palm. (Fig. 251)

(2) Turn the toes of the left foot outward, continue to turn the body to the left, bend the left knee and straighten the right leg naturally. At the same time, continue to swing the left palm to the left and raise the left palm horizontally symmetrical to the right palm on the two sides, elbow slightly bent and both palms forward. Look at the left palm. (Fig. 252)

(3) Shift the weight to the right, toes of the left foot turned inward, and turn the body to the right. Move both palms downward and inward in arcs and cross them at the wrists in front of the abdomen (left palm outside) and raise them to the front of the chest, both palms inward. Look forward. (Fig. 253)

Fig. 251

Fig. 252

Fig. 253

(4) Withdraw the left foot to keep the feet parallel and a shoulder width apart, toes of both feet forward. Then straighten both legs and turn the upper body upright. Keep the palms crossed and raise them in front of the chest at shoulder level, arms forming a circle, left palm outside. Look forward. (Fig. 254)

Points for attention: When swinging the palms to the left, keep the toes of the right foot pointing due south, and turn the left foot gradually outward as the body turns and the weight is shifted to the left. When the hands are crossed, first turn the toes of the left foot inward and then withdraw the left foot before raising the body slowly. Turn the waist back gently until it faces due south. Keep the weight between the legs.

Closing Form

(1) Turn the forearms inward simultaneously and move the palms to a shoulder width apart, palms down, and lower them slowly. Look forward. (Fig. 255)

(2) Drop the hands slowly to both sides of the legs. Keep the

upper body upright and the head slightly raised. Relax the shoulders, drop the elbows, breathe naturally, and Look forward. (Fig. 256)

(3) Move the left foot back to the right foot, feet together and toes forward. Look forward. (Fig. 257)

Points for attention: Concentration of mind, tempo of movements, and exertion of force should be even and complete throughout the exercise. Keep the body natural and firm.

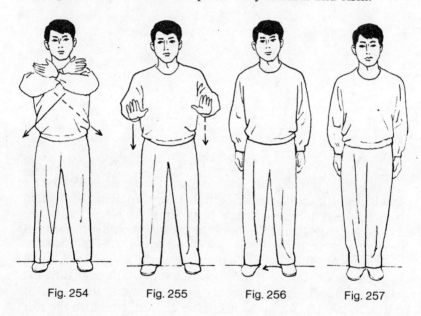

Fig. 254   Fig. 255   Fig. 256   Fig. 257

V. Diagram of the Lines of Movements

Starting Form
White Crane Spreads Its Wings
Brush Knee with Bow Step, Left
Single Whip, Left
Hand Strums Lute, Left
Stroke and Push (One)
Stroke and Push (Two)
Stroke and Push (Three)
Turn to Strike, Parry and Punch, Left
Ward off, Stroke, Push and Press, Left
Lean Obliquely
Punch Under Elbow
Step Back and Whirl Arms on Both Sides (One)
Step Back and Whirl Arms on Both Sides (Two)
Step Back and Whirl Arms on Both Sides (Three)
Step Back and Whirl Arms on Both Sides (Four)
Turn to Push Palms (One)
Turn to Push Palms (Two)
Turn to Push Palms (Three)
Turn to Push Palms (Four)
Hand Strums Lute, Right
Brush Knee and Punch Downward
White Snake Sticks Out Its Tongue (One)
White Snake Sticks Out Its Tongue (Two)
Pat Foot to Subdue Tiger (One)
Pat Foot to Subdue Tiger (Two)
Turn Left to Strike
Thread Palm on Crouch Stance
Ward off on One Leg (One)
Ward off on One Leg (Two)
Single Whip, Right

Wave Hands like Clouds (One)
Wave Hands like Clouds (Two)
Wave Hands like Clouds (Three)
Part Horse's Mane on Right Side
Part Horse's Mane on Left Side
Pat High on Horse
Kick with Right Heel
Strike Opponent's Ears with Both Fists
Kick with Left Heel
Strike with Hidden Fist
Needle at Sea Bottom
Flash Arm
Kick with Right Foot
Kick with Left Foot
Brush Knee with Bow Step (One)
Brush Knee with Bow Step (Two)
Step Forward to Strike
Apparent Close-Up
Wave Hands like Clouds (One)
Wave Hands like Clouds (Two)
Wave Hands like Clouds (Three)
Turn Right to Strike, Right
Work at Shuttles on Left Side
Work at Shuttles on Right Side
Step Back and Thread Palm
Press Down Palms on Empty Step
Stand on One Leg and Hold out Palm
Push Forearm with Horse-Riding Step
Turn Body with Big Strokes
Swing Palm with Crouch Step
Step Forward to Cross Fists
Stand on One Leg to Mount Tiger
Turn Body for Lotus Leg Swing
Draw Bow to Shoot Tiger
Turn to Strike, Parry and Punch, Right
Ward off, Stroke, Push and Press, Right
Cross Hands

Closing Form

Notes:
1. The entire set of exercises is indicated on one straight line. Since it is impossible to write all the words in one place, the diagram is extended.

2. If several movements are executed in the same place, the names of the exercises are listed together.

3. The bottom line of the name of the exercise is the direction the practitioner faces and the top line is the direction of the back of the practitioner.

4. In the diagram, it is imagined that the direction the practitioner faces to begin is south.

Starting Form

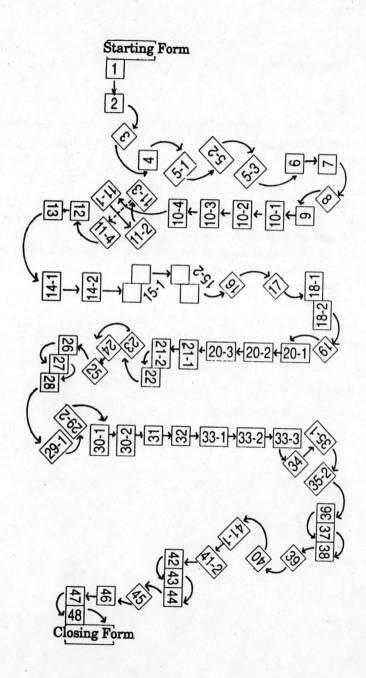

Closing Form